CHILDREN

MEAN THE WORLD

TO GOD

D1418050

The profound importance of children
in your life, your congregation, your world

DR. HAROLD SHANK

Play-Doh Globe Photograph: Rupert Yen, Memphis
Engraving: Rudolph Hirsch & Company, Memphis
Family photo: David Ralston, Memphis
Cover design: Trace Hallowell of Tactical Magic, Memphis

Table of Contents

Preface

Do you remember the people who helped you as a child? You may recall that kind uncle or pleasant second grade teacher or a generous older sister who gave you advice or guided you through a problem or brought you gifts. I imagine you're thankful for what they did.

In a similar way I would like to recognize those who influenced the writing of this book about children. Many have offered advice like that kind uncle. Included among their number are Carisse Berryhill, Michelle Betts, Buster Clemens, Trace Hallowell, Sue Henderson, John Mark Hicks, David Ralston, Vernon Ray, and Marcella Trevathan. The people of Christian Child and Family Services Association and the staff at 21st Century Christian must also be acknowledged for their outstanding counsel.

Three people have been like that second grade teacher pulling me through problems that at times looked insurmountable. Chris Altrock, David Jordan, and Wayne Reed helped me overcome obstacles along the way.

Those closest to me have played the role of the generous older sister. My wife, Sally, is a gift from God, and her insights are found on every page. I'm grateful to her and our sons, Daniel and Nathan, for giving us all the gift of their experiences.

I found it necessary in this book to share memories from my own childhood and in the process I have exposed the lives of my parents to you. I'm grateful for their support and affection. What a blessing they gave me in life! To honor and thank them, I dedicate this book to my father and mother, Leroy and Florence Shank.

No one has more influence on all of us than our Heavenly Father. My greatest hope is that this study will glorify him by motivating us to do his will.

Harold Shank
Memphis, Tennessee
May 11, 2001

Introduction
You Can Make a Difference

This book is about children, but not for children. It's not a manual for teachers on how to work with children or for parents on how to raise kids. It's for all adults, even those without children. It's for all people, but especially those who follow Jesus. Especially you.

It's a book about God's view of children. It's a call to understand that if children mean the world to God, then those of you in the church must regard children the way God does. By changing the way the church treats children, you reshape the future. Through children God has given you the opportunity today to transform tomorrow's world.

This book is challenging, inspiring, and hopeful. While there is much here that will challenge us, it tells the stories of people who have found their faith deepened by understanding what God is doing with children. I hope that by thinking biblically with me, you will realize more completely the work God has called us to do.

All is not well with children. Children are in crisis. My heart is troubled by what I have seen and heard. At first I didn't believe, and for a long time I was afraid to act. But now I am convinced, and now I speak. Here is a sample of what I've seen and heard.

Children in Crisis

Mel and Meg Johnson have two children, Tracy and Terry. From the outside they seem to be a close-knit family, but Mel is obsessed with softball. He plays on three softball teams, coaches another, and referees for two recreational leagues. He works all day as a programmer for a local electronics company which allows the family to live well, but evenings and weekends are taken up with softball.

Meg complains to Mel that the kids are growing up without a father. She told a friend in her Sunday school class that she sometimes feels like a single mom. Tracy, a seventh grader, recently drew a picture of a puzzle with a piece missing and showed it to her Sunday school teacher. She colored the empty spot black, said it was a self-portrait. She felt as though she had a hole in her heart because she never saw her Daddy.

Mary and Kimberly are bright and attractive, both heavily involved in their senior high school activities. They joined the same club in their sophomore year. The exclusive group catered to teens who could afford nice clothes and expensive outings. Parents pressured the girls to look good and to maintain a certain image. Attendance at club activities was mandatory. With school work, and their youth group at church, all the activity became too much for them to handle.

They thought that dropping out of the club would end the pressure, but they found themselves ostracized by their peers, criticized by adults, and even penalized by their school. The whole experience discouraged both girls. Mary cried herself to sleep for a month afterward. Kimberly wondered if she had done the right thing by dropping out of the club. She felt like there was no one she could really talk to about her problem.

Marty's dad worked for one of the expanding hi-tech companies. They moved when he was in fifth grade and again during his seventh grade year. Each time Marty found it a struggle to make new friends. When the company moved them to Memphis during the summer prior to his freshman year in high school, Marty dreaded the whole process. They bought a nice house in the suburbs and he enrolled in an academically elite high school.

Nobody at the new school wanted to be his friend. In seventh grade he had been accepted by some students in his math class, but at the Memphis school all the guys in his algebra class already had friends. At lunch he found three boys, Wade, Stephen, and Benjamin, who spent the weekends drinking together at Wade's house because his parents were always gone. Soon Marty's life was dominated by alcohol. The move to Memphis fueled his dad's career, but brought Marty's life to a standstill.

When the visitors to the maternity section of a Memphis hospital looked at all the newborns, April got as many oohs and aahs as the others. She had a cute little nose and black hair. But April's life soon took a negative turn. Her two older sisters already lived with other family members because her mother's career interfered with child raising. Sharon was a prostitute.

About the time April started to crawl, Sharon went to prison for a three-year term for soliciting an undercover police officer. From prison Sharon tried to keep up with her baby, but people don't return phone calls to the women's lockup. Letters with a return address that includes "Detention Center" are not high priority. During the three years Sharon was in prison, mother and daughter had no contact. April became somebody else's little girl.

Anthony and I went to visit four sisters whose mother, Stacey, had just died of AIDS. Stacey had been a faithful Christian woman whose promiscuous husband had infected her with that deadly disease. The chaos in the family had thrown them into deep poverty. Two of the four sisters had babies of their own. The six lived in a dirty shotgun house in the center city.

As we ministered to the sisters, I watched the two babies on the rough wood floor try repeatedly to get the attention of their distracted mothers. Finally, one gave up and found a pile of dirt in the corner. I watched her examine it. In the middle of the pile were several cast off pieces of cold meat. The little one reached out and grabbed a piece. Before I could move, she had popped it into her mouth.

The list goes on. Children in our world are being crushed. Kids are crying out in pain. What I have seen with my own eyes and heard with my own ears is echoed in what others are saying about the state of today's children.

I've agonized over how to begin this book. I want to bring hope not hurt, solutions not scowls, optimism not offense. Yet we cannot study what God has to say about children and our role with children until we have a common starting place about the state of children. The bookstores and magazine racks are filled with statements of the issues facing kids today. Five broad trends are hurting our children.

(1) *A crisis exists in the family.* Increasing numbers of children face the loss of at least one parent. Fathers walk out on their children. Mothers desert their little ones. Even in homes with both parents, kids run away or face mothers or fathers who are substance abusers or so preoccupied with their own problems they have no time for their own offspring. Sexual, physical and verbal abuse of children has reached an alarming state. Too many children come home from school to an empty house. Too many parents work such long hours during the week that they only see their kids on weekends. In our homes, we are often too busy for our own children. We put them in front of television or let them play video games for hours. Many parents see their children being pressured and overloaded with activities but feel helpless to stop the process. Even in the best of homes children are often lonely and troubled.

(2) *The once safe environment of school has been threatened.* School systems are under-funded. Teachers pass failing children on to the next grade because they really don't want them for a second go-around. Students go to class wondering who is pack-

ing a gun or carrying a knife. Schools start earlier and stay open later than ever before because kids need a place to be. Children feel pressure to achieve high standards set by coaches, teachers and upwardly mobile parents who want their children to go beyond what they themselves have done. Most parents have been dismayed by events in their child's school. Most of us worry about sending children off to class and what changes the educational process will ultimately bring for good or bad to our child. Every ineffective teacher, each unfair exam, every playground bully makes us realize how lonely and fearful children often feel at school.

(3) *The media put children at risk*. Children see things that were once only available to adult eyes. Little ones must make decisions that they have not been taught to make about things they are not prepared to see as they surf the internet. Decision-makers in media and the business world target children with products that are great profit-makers, but do little to provide a nurturing environment for children. It seems that every time we rent a video for our family there is something offensive that invades our family room. Many parents cringe at the content of commercials and the language of prime time shows. Trying to sort out the constant barrage of the media only intensifies the feelings of isolation and confusion in children.

(4) *The moral standards of America threaten children*. In Shelby County, where I live, half of the children born each year are born out of wedlock. Many of those children are shuffled from one relative to another. There are ten thousand children in our state that have been deserted by their parents. Teen preg-

nancy, venereal disease, drug use, and alcoholism have all taken their toll. Everyday children are shot and killed with guns in America. Every hour children are sexually abused by adults. Children become aware of the conflicting standards of morality at an early age. Even in elementary school, adolescents must make decisions. Children who hear adults talking about cheating on income taxes or manipulating a neighbor into moving a fence, or who see the family take personal advantage of a situation, must sort out what is right all by themselves. Confusion and fear fill their minds.

(5) *Economic structures work against children.* One of every four American children is born poor. Nearly nine million American children live in families that receive public assistance. Over a half million children are in foster care nationwide. Every single day 34,000 children die in the world from starvation and easily-cured childhood diseases.[1] The world economy has also brought affluence to many homes. Children growing up in freshly built subdivisions with shiny new cars in the driveway and the best of clothes in the closet are confronted with issues of greed and selfishness. Such contexts create confusion for children who are trying, often alone, to sort out what is significant in their lives.

A Call to Action

We all see children crying for help. My purpose is not to examine the problem, but to consider solutions. My mission is

[1]For these and other statistics about the dangers facing today's children see: Ron Sider, *Rich Christians in An Age of Hunger* (Dallas: Word, 1997), pp 1-19. Cf. an associated web site: www.ESA-online.org. *The State of America's Children Yearbook* (Washington, DC: Children's Defense Fund, 1999), pp 1-30. Cf. their web site: www.childrensdefense.org. *Kids Count Data Book* (Baltimore, MD: The Annie E. Casey Foundation, 1999), pp 1-15. Cf. their web site: www.aecf.org. Also see *Child Welfare League of America* web site: www.cwla.org.

not to look at causes, but to propose remedies. My desire is not to focus on what is wrong with our world, or sick in our society, but to lead us to what is right and healthy for our children.

I write to the church. I maintain that God calls his people to be intimately involved with the children in their midst and in the larger community, and that, through the church, God broadcasts his own concerns about children. My goal is to explain the biblical doctrines behind what we already do with children and the biblical demands for what we should be doing better. This book will indict any church or any spiritual leader who neglects the biblical teaching about children, provide a rallying point around which the church can gather volunteers to serve children, and call the church to action. The first four chapters examine the basic biblical foundations for thinking about children. Chapters five through nine present ways the church should minister to children. The final four chapters show how God's church tells the world his heart's concerns for children.

I am calling you and your church to change the way you treat children. I am calling us to pay more attention to the youth in our midst, in our communities, and in our world. This is not my call, but a biblical vision. Children mean the world to God. This book is a call to hear their cries, and share God's heart for children, and by changing children, to change the world.

Chapter One
Hear the Cry

Hear A Child

Anyone observing me when I was twelve years old would not have suspected the turmoil on the inside. I was trying to find God. Our family was totally unchurched. My only church experience came from the two Vacation Bible Schools I attended each summer. One was at the Church of the Brethren. They met in the basement under the music store on Main Street in our mid-sized town. The disabled woman who played the piano always wore a smile. Her lively playing still echoes in my ears. Every summer the Brethren invited us to VBS. My two oldest sisters and I would go. Every year that was it. Nothing more from the Church of the Brethren until next summer. I felt forgotten.

The other VBS was at the Church of Christ located at the end of our street. They had better cookies than the Brethren and had more fun. The leader of the VBS would hide each day's attendance figure at a different place at the front of their church building. We stayed up at night thinking about where he would hide the numbers the next day. Every summer the Church of Christ invited us to VBS. My two oldest sisters and I would go. Every year that was it. Nothing more from the Church of Christ until next summer. My feelings of being forgotten intensified.

Trying to Find God

By the time I was twelve, I knew enough about God from VBS to yearn for more, but I didn't know what to do. I hadn't read the Bible. I had no churchgoing adults to imitate. It was a long time until the next VBS. And VBS was such a busy time that I wasn't sure it was appropriate to raise my questions about God. My confusion and isolation made me wonder where all this God-stuff would lead me.

I remember feeling very alone in the whole matter.

ⓒ ⓑ

This Child Means the World to God

When Josh was fourteen, he ran away from his suburban home for the third time. His mother called the church so we started making calls and soon found him at the home of a school friend where he was deep into a video game. He was running from an alcoholic mother who struggled desperately to keep the family together. In seventh grade, Josh made straight A's. This year he's averaging a C minus. When I see him in the hallways at church he's rather quiet, but inside Josh is crying out for help.

The questions about God were so hard to answer. I wanted somebody to teach me, to help me understand what I was supposed to do. All the adults around me either seemed to have no interest in these questions or no interest in me. It was as though I had been taken to the front door of the house, put outside, and told I was on my own. I felt forgotten. Anybody with a box of religious answers would probably have satisfied my curiosity and answered my questions. I could easily have become a Jew or a Muslim or a Catholic. But none of them had Vacation Bible School.

The world is filled with children who are just like I was: children who are lonely and confused, children with unanswered questions and spiritual yearnings, children searching for God all by themselves. Some of these children may come from unchurched homes, but many of them already attend our congregations and are growing up in our midst. Being a child can be an intensely lonely experience, especially when it comes to spiritual issues.

All of this raises questions for me as a Christian. What does the Bible say about lonely children? Do Christian people have any role to play in the issues facing troubled kids? What do we in the churches need to understand about God and ourselves that can help us make a difference in the lives of these children?

Hear God's Heart

One of the first troubled children in the Bible was the oldest son of Abraham. Ishmael's story is told in Genesis 16-25. Here is the big picture: Early in Genesis, God chooses Abraham as the means by which he will bless the world. God decides to do that by giving blessings to Abraham's offspring. When his wife remains barren, the whole promise is put in jeopardy. As the events unfold, Abraham ends up with two boys, Isaac and Ishmael. This is the story of Ishmael.

When Abraham and Sarah did not receive the promised child, Sarah took matters into her own hands by arranging for Abraham to have offspring by her Egyptian handmaiden, Hagar (Genesis 16). Hagar conceived. Instead of pleasing Sarah, Hagar's pregnancy elicited scorn. "Then Sarai mistreated Hagar; so she fled from her" (Genesis 16:6).

Exile in the wilderness complicated Hagar's pregnancy. God appeared to Hagar with a prediction about the unborn child, "He will be a wild donkey of a man; his hand will be against everyone and everyone's hand against him, and he will live in hostility toward all his brothers" (Genesis 16:12). No mother-to-be wants to hear that kind of news, or be homeless during pregnancy, or bear a child that nobody wants. Yet, despite Sarah's crushing behavior, and the problematic prediction about his life, Ishmael was born when Abraham was eighty-six (Genesis 16:16).

The Genesis events are not told from Ishmael's point of view. The focus of the story is on God's redemptive plan which would deliver a great blessing to all humans through the line of Abraham. Not every descendant of Abraham would carry that blessing. The ones who did not carry the blessing were not insignificant or disposable, they were just not part of that prom-ised line. The Genesis text does not say when Ishmael learned of this great plan of God. We do not get any information about how he responded when he learned that his father was chosen by God to bring the world a great blessing and that the blessing would be passed on through his son. Nor do we know when Ishmael realized that he would *not* be the one to carry the blessing. Because Ishmael was not the chosen son, he enters the story briefly and then exits. After Genesis 25, the Bible has little interest in Ishmael or his descendants. But before he leaves we learn something critical about God's attitude toward Ishmael.

When Isaac was born, God made it clear that he was the boy to carry on Abraham's work. Abraham and Sarah were delighted to finally have the baby God promised. The celebration over Isaac is described in Genesis 21. The promised boy had arrived. Isaac would carry the blessing of God to the next generation.

Get Rid of Him

Now we know that Ishmael knows. If it was not completely evident to this fourteen-year-old that his baby brother is the promised child, it becomes clear as Genesis 21 unfolds. Seeking to join in the party, Ishmael played with his baby brother. When Sarah saw the two boys together, she was upset. Given her hostility toward Hagar years before, we can only suspect the ongoing problems that existed in this complex family unit. Sarah went straight to Abraham to demand that something be done with Ishmael. She insisted that he not be involved in their future. "Get rid of that slave woman and her son, for that slave woman's son will never share in the inheritance with my son Isaac" (Genesis 21:10). How much of this conversation Ishmael heard, we do not know. Since Sarah had maintained her animosity against Hagar for fourteen years, we can only imagine the details of Ishmael's unfortunate childhood.

Abraham was upset by Sarah's request. Apparently, unlike his wife, he had developed deep feelings for his oldest boy. "The matter distressed Abraham greatly because it concerned his son" (Genesis 21:11). God counseled Abraham to send the boy and his mother away. The promised line cannot be challenged in any way.

We may wonder about God's actions toward this teenager. Did he not care? How can we adore a God who casts out teenagers? How are we to make sense of the turmoil in this family caused in part by the promise God made to bless the world through Abraham's lineage? The story gets worse.

What follows is the result of family jealousy and sibling rivalry. The family problems boiled over. Something had to be done. The father decided. The two had to leave. The scene at the door took place in response to Sarah's insistence that the house wasn't big enough for baby Isaac and teenage Ishmael. Somebody had to go, and it wasn't going to be her. Abraham was forced to send Hagar and Ishmael away.

With nothing but the shirts on their backs and the bags in their hands, the boy and his mother left to find a new life. But the world is a wilderness for a single mother and a child, more desolate than most of us understand. Nothing seemed to work out right. Every road seemed to be a dead end. Nobody was willing to help.

All Alone

When the food was eaten and the water was gone, with no oasis or friendly caravan nearby, Hagar despaired. She cried out in pain. The only option was to desert the boy. Her only protection was to get far away from him so she would not have to witness his final breath or hear his bitter cries. So Hagar put Ishmael under a bush, moved away, and wept. Ishmael, apparently too weak from hunger and dehydration to return to his mother, whimpered in his final moments. She couldn't look. She turned away. She couldn't protect him from the hot sun of burning reality, so she left him in a patch of shade next to a desert road. With no money, no food, no housing, no support, no job, no future, there was nothing else to do.

Sent away by his father, abandoned by his mother, the fourteen-year-old cried. In fact, both mother and son wept. Mother crying because she could not mother her child, grieved at the possibility that the one she had brought into the world would soon be leaving the world, anguished at the life ebbing away in the nearby shadows. Son weeping because he was now all alone. Unable to care for himself, vulnerable in the hostile environment, he awaited what no young person should have to contemplate, death as a child.

Ishmael heads a long line of lonely, crying children. As we read the story we wonder if anybody besides Hagar knows what the boy is facing. Is there anyone to share his burden? Will someone wipe away the tears? Does anyone hear the cry?

"God heard the boy crying" (Genesis 21:17).

In the midst of the crying someone heard. There was a response. The one who heard the boy cry was God. Of all the prayers and all the noise of earth that came into his heavenly throne room that day, this one boy's cries were heard. God heard the cry that Hagar heard and moved to help Hagar comfort that cry. God heard the cry and did what Hagar could not do.

All that from Ishmael. What an interesting name. It's not one that we typically use to name our male offspring in western culture. I suspect there are not many Ishmaels in your church. There are none in ours. In fact, I don't know a person named Ishmael. In many ways it's too bad that the name Ishmael is not used in our society, not just because it was the name of a boy whose cry was heard by God, but because the name Ishmael has an interesting history. *Ishmael is a Hebrew word that means, "God hears."*

Hear The Call

We might want to dismiss this story because Ishmael was not in the chosen line. We pay attention to the chosen son, thinking that he is the only one who matters. But the son not chosen also mattered to God. God paid attention to the boy who was not the son of the promise. He was not the one marked to carry God's blessing. Ishmael was the result of Sarah's plan to accomplish what she thought God was unable to do. Ishmael, the other son. Ishmael, the disposable child. Ishmael, the vulnerable. Ishmael, the lonely. Given Ishmael's unimportance in the grand scheme of things, it is particularly striking that God hears his cry.

Somebody's Listening

I find great comfort in the story because, in the grand scheme of things, I was not an important child. My parents didn't go to church. I didn't know the Bible stories. I didn't understand prayer. I was confused about God. Ishmael's pain reminds me of my own.

I find great comfort in God hearing Ishmael because I believe God heard me. If God heard Ishmael, a tangent in the Genesis story, and if God heard me, a boy who didn't go to church, then there is somebody listening to the lonely, vulnerable children in this world.

Genesis 21 raises an image of God that we often overlook. It is a God who seeks out a lonely child and takes care of him. This story provides a model of a caring God interacting with a lonely, vulnerable child. It tells us children mean the world to God. As we seek to be like God, we, too, must hear the lonely and seek out the vulnerable. We find in God's hearing the cry of Ishmael, the kind of concern we should show and the kind of role we should play in the lives of children. God did not leave this child alone and did not leave us without a model of how to respond to these children.

The Genesis 21 story is not unique in Scripture. God repeatedly hears the cries of children. God heard Abel's blood cry out from the ground. God responded to teenaged Joseph in the pit and in prison. He listened to the pleas of the children of Israel in Egypt. The cries of the deserted baby in the basket floating on the Nile were noted in heaven. God heard young Samuel in the tabernacle, and the teenager David before his fight with Goliath, and the virgin Mary as she responded to Gabriel. When Jesus told his parable of the prodigal son, he described a waiting father who listened to the cries of both boys. The prodigal son's father reveals that God is filled with welcome, compassion, grace, forgiveness, and joy for his children. God hears the cry of children.

We live in a time of crisis for children. Our neighborhoods are filled with children whose parents don't have time for them. Lonely children turn to violence, drugs, and sex to fill the void. Yet their cries, like the cry of Ishmael, do not go unheard. God hears the cries of these children. Do we?

The loving, caring, compassionate God that we have come to value as adults is also concerned about children. God's relationship with people does not wait until they reach adulthood. Given these texts, we cannot exclude children from the biblical teaching about God. For most of my adult life, I thought the central concern of God, and thus of the church, was adults. I was wrong. The same God who called the adult Abraham heard a teenager named Ishmael. When Jesus wanted to describe the nature of his father, he pictured him as a father who deeply loved his two sons. To be like God we must be as concerned about children as he is. To be his people we must train ourselves to hear the cry of lonely children just as our God hears their cries. We adults must include children in our biblical thinking, in our church decisions, and in our understanding of who God is.

It's not right for children to be alone.

It's not right for children to be ignored.

It's not right for children to be treated unfairly.

It's not right for children to be forced into the adult world.

It's not right for children to be left out of the church's vision.

It's not right for children to be alone in their search for God.

Children are not peripheral to the heart of God. They must not be peripheral to the ministry of the church.

How Mildred Changed My Life, and Yours

I never ran away from home, but I readily identify with Ishmael's loneliness, vulnerability and despair. The confusion mounted in my mind throughout my sixth grade year. Finally the Church of Christ VBS came around again. The teacher was a nice gray-haired woman named Mildred Stutzman. After VBS, Mildred took me aside. I couldn't figure out why she wanted to talk to me. I was just a little kid from the neighborhood who went to VBS every summer. She explained that she also had a sixth grade class on Sunday morning. It met in the same room. Some of the same children that were in VBS were in her class. She invited me to attend.

I remember being amazed at what Mildred was asking. In the grand scheme of things I wasn't important. I was the naive child who never went to church. But I was struggling with the God question, wondering where I would get answers. Then came a voice asking me to come to a place where those questions might be discussed. God heard my cry. He answered it with Mildred Stutzman.

The next Sunday she introduced me to Abraham, Ishmael's dad. What a journey we had. Every Sunday morning we would sing "When He Cometh" and then open our quarterlies to read about Abraham. I filled out every blank in that book. I'd never heard of these stories before, ever. Abraham believed in God. In Abraham's life I began to see the answer to the questions that I had about God. I don't remember reading much about Ishmael. That would have made this chapter better if I could tell you that I really identified with Ishmael when I was twelve, but I guess I forced him out of my memory just like his dad had forced him out of the house.

So I started going to Sunday school and staying for church. Church was good for me. There I learned not just about Abraham and his descendants, but about Jesus and his family. It became clear to me that the invitation was always open to become part of Jesus' family. If I became part of God's people then I'd never be alone in my search for him.

Two years later, with a great deal of thinking about the God-stuff in between, I told the preacher, "This is what I want. I want Jesus in my life and I want my life in this church." I became a Christian. But I never could get Abraham out of my system. Eventually I learned Hebrew, the original language of Genesis, and went on to do a doctorate in biblical studies. If you look up my dissertation at the library, you'll find it under "Genesis." I think Mildred would have been proud.

Will You Be Like Mildred?

Mildred heard the cry of one spiritually lonely child. By giving attention to that boy, she was the conduit by which God changed his life. By listening to one child, Mildred set in motion a series of events that have influenced many people, including you as you read this book. When we change the way we treat children, we change the world.

Two lonely kids. Both finally rescued. Nothing has been more significant to me than hearing that voice in the wilderness of my life. Nothing is more important than the sense that God was waiting compassionately for me. Nothing is more important for all the world's lonely, vulnerable, and hurting children, than hearing some voice, some affirmation, in the time of their wilderness journey. It is not simply a matter of teaching children about God, but of hearing their cries. For some it may be guiding them to water as God did with Ishmael, or giving them the robe as the father did with the prodigal, or leading them to Scripture as Mildred did with me. To see that we in the church do not forget about the lonely children is a mission to which I am called. And that is why I write this book.

Exercises

Hear A Child

1. Recall a time in your childhood when you faced crisis. How did you feel? Did anyone intercede? What was the outcome?

2. In small groups tell about children you know who are facing difficult situations. As each person shares, list the children's names and their difficulties. Pray about each.

Hear God's Heart

3. List other children mentioned in Genesis. What indications are there about their isolation as children?

4. Reread Genesis 16-25. List all the times God interacted with Hagar and Ishmael.

Hear the Call

5. Make a list of all the children's ministries in your church. Pray through the list, giving thanks for these ministries and leaders.

6. Share about situations where Christians stepped in to make a difference in a child's life.

7. What can you do this week to encourage a hurting child or teen?

Chapter Two
Helping Every Child Feel Good

Hear A Child

As a child I was teased about our house. One of my classmates in seventh grade, Ted Moss, called it a Quonset hut. He told other kids at school that we lived in an army surplus building. I never knew what a Quonset hut was, but I hated the story Ted told. He was spreading that story about the same time I was searching for God. I wondered if God would be interested in a boy from a Quonset hut.

An Unhappy Boy from an Ugly House

Ted had reason to tell his story. My parents bought a plain house. Over the next decade my father worked at night and every weekend to transform it into a sprawling split level. In between it was ugly. When we put the addition on the front, we put the I-beam first. For months there was a twenty-foot long I-beam sticking out of the front of the house. I always thought it looked like the house was sticking its tongue out at passers-by. I wondered who wanted to be friends with a boy who lived in a house like that?

☙ ❧

This Child
Means the World
to God

Joey started attending church with his mother. We quickly learned that there were problems at home. One day when services were over, I saw Joey playing with my son, Daniel. They were both about five. I called, "Son, it's time to go." When Daniel got up to follow me, his blond-haired friend grabbed my coat. "Mister, mister, why did you call that boy 'Son?'" At first I didn't understand. Then I realized that this little guy had never had a parent call him "Son."

The worst thing about the house was that I had to work on it. While other kids were playing ball or visiting at each other's houses, I had to help my dad. For several years we spent evenings bricking the house. My job was to mix the cement and haul it to my dad. The worst part was the bricks. We bought all the bricks at once and piled them on the ground in the front yard. The bricks were white, but the ground was dirty. Every single brick had to be scrubbed and cleaned before it could be put on the house. Every night I scrubbed bricks. I hated bricks. Washing bricks was a lonely job. As I scrubbed, I thought about how alone I was and how my friends were playing baseball or having fun at each other's houses.

As an adult I am amazed that I remember such feelings so clearly and that I knew where I stood in the grand scheme of things. I also recall my inability to deal with those feelings, the lack of clarity I felt about my own future, the uncertainty about my own worth. I needed something, but I had no idea what. I felt that I was missing something, but I couldn't verbalize what it was. All I knew was that at times I felt unwanted.

Feel Their Pain

Being a child in our society is often a lonely, fearful and uncertain experience. Many children feel unwanted. I remember the sense that nobody wanted me. When I listen to the music sung by today's teenagers, I hear the same message. All of us know that the adult notion that "nobody cares" has its roots deep in childhood. Young people often sense that nobody cares about them. They do not feel loved or accepted. In their search for God, they don't know where to turn because nobody seems to be willing to listen. Too many children feel the pain of Ishmael: rejected by his father, deserted by his mother, left to die under a bush by a society that had the resources to save him, but simply did not care.

Disregarded children miss out on many things. If children do not get some sense of affection, appreciation and acceptance, they struggle the rest of their lives. Many problems faced by adults have their roots in the lack of those things as children. When they spend excessive time by themselves, they are not developing relationships with adults, not learning to communicate, not understanding the fundamentals of life. They are mal-nourished spiritually and emotionally. They do not receive affec-tion, guidance, and teaching. They hear messages from the media, school, and peers, but those lack the substance and spir-itual richness that they need.

Many neglected children are not hugged and touched. Because of abuse and lawsuits, many are now afraid to touch children. Educators are concerned about the legal complications of what a teacher is to do when a child comes up and hugs them. Separated from busy parents, isolated from other children by playing video games or surfing the internet, and distanced from untouching teachers, children struggle to understand their intense feelings of loneliness.

As a result children cry out in the only way they can. They do things that hurt themselves. They try drugs. They resort to vio-lence. They fail school. They turn against authority. They live a virtual life on the internet. They find make-believe friendships in far away musicians who sing words that make sense to their troubled lives.

How do we give children the spiritual nourishment, the rela-tionships they need in our high tech, fast-paced life? What kind of acceptance do the children around us find? What can we do to make children feel wanted?

Hear God's Heart

I believe the fundamental responses of Christian people are tied up in two words that carry much doctrinal and practical freight in Scripture. I believe that the God who heard Ishmael's cry acted in these two ways toward Ishmael, and that beyond Ishmael God wants us to respond to all people, but especially to all children in these two fundamental ways. The two words that explain this biblical teaching are *blessing* and *gospel*. These two interrelated ideas represent God's holistic response to humanity and to children.

Blessing has a focus on this world, *gospel* on the next. *Blessing* centers on the good physical things of this life, *gospel* focuses on the good spiritual things of this life. God wants us to be safe (*blessing*) and saved (*gospel*). He desires us to be joyful and heaven-bound. He wants us to feel acceptance and assurance. While I do not maintain that *blessing* and *gospel* are mutually exclusive or that those words appear everywhere a troubled child is mentioned in Scripture, I believe the substance of these two teachings is at the core of how we as a church should think about children. I will take up *blessing* in this chapter and *gospel* in the next.

What is Blessing?

Blessing has seldom taken on a major theological role among Christians. In the dictionary of theological terms in one of the most widely used Bible handbooks currently available, the word "blessing" does not even make the list. We have pushed blessing aside. We think that what Jesus was doing to children when he blessed them was cute or nice, but not theological or doctrinal. We write volumes on baptism, we preach sermons on grace, and we sing songs about love, but we do little serious reflection about blessing, a word that appears regularly in the Bible. We stress the core biblical doctrines that all adults must come to understand, but generally ignore this one central doctrine about children.

When it comes to children, Christians often look first to education or psychology for answers rather than Scripture. We know about teachable moments, adolescence, SIDS, ADD, ADHD, self-esteem, and puberty, but have not thought seriously about what it means to bless a child. Cultural dictates about children typically take precedence over biblical mandates. We insist that children be safe, well-educated, and properly clothed, but few churches insist that the children entrusted to them be blessed.

Part of our lack of emphasis on blessing is due to the complex nature of the biblical teaching about blessing. The word blessing has three different meanings in Scripture. First, the word blessing means to *worship.* Humans throughout Scripture offer their blessings to God. For example, when Zechariah, the father of John the Baptist, regained his voice, "he began to speak, praising God" (Luke 1:64). The word "praising" is actually the word "bless." Bless means to speak well of, or to bow down in front of, or simply to worship (see Psalm 28:6).

Second, the word blessing means to *receive good things from God.* In Genesis 1:22 God blessed the birds and fishes indicating that he wants the best possible world for them. At the other end of the Bible God blesses those dressing for eternity, showing his intention of giving them good things forever (Revelation 22:14). This concept of blessing appears frequently in Scripture (cf. Deuteronomy 28:1-14; Psalms1:1; 5:12; 128; 144; Matthew 5:3-12).

Third, blessing refers to the role we play in *passing the good things of God on to other people.* This meaning of blessing is an extension of the second one. God wants to give us good things. Sometimes those good things are from the hand of God himself.

Other times they come through another person. In the Bible the blessings of God were passed on by parents (Genesis 27; 48; 49), priests (Numbers 6:24-26), kings (2 Samuel 6:18), and apostles (Ephesians 1:3).

All three meanings of blessing are shown in bold type in the Genesis text about Melchizedek.

> After Abram returned from defeating Kedorlaomer and the kings allied with him, the king of Sodom came out to meet him in the Valley of Shaveh (that is, the King's Valley). Then Melchizedek king of Salem brought out bread and wine. He was priest of God Most High, and he **blessed** Abram, saying, "**Blessed** be Abram by God Most High, Creator of heaven and earth. And **blessed** be God Most High, who delivered your enemies into your hand." Then Abram gave him a tenth of everything (Genesis 14:17-20).

In the third occurrence here Melchizedek blesses God. That is the blessing or worship humans give to God. In such cases the original word for "blessing" is often translated as "praise." When humans bless God they are worshiping. The second blessing in Genesis 14 comes from God to Abram. That is the blessing that comes from God to people or objects on the earth. The first mention of blessing here flows from Melchizedek to Abram. This blessing is from one human to another.

Giving Good Things

To bless means to give prosperity and goodness. It has to do with physical success and long life. It means to live a fortunate and happy life. It means to feel accepted and wanted. It has the idea of being linked to other significant people. When God blesses people, he is expressing his solidarity with them. When one individual blesses another, he is conveying something of his interest in the other's well-being. Blessing means to speak well of, to be for another, to wish another the goodness of life.

Blessing is not limited to physical happiness or material prosperity, but includes all spiritual blessings as well. The word appears in each of the beatitudes in Matthew 5 signifying the great spiritual depth of blessing. The great Aaronic blessing in Numbers 6 ("the LORD bless you and keep you. . . .") are words that offer us deep emotional and spiritual assurance.

Blessing is so wide in its scope that we may not even see it. Blessing is to the individual what air is to the lungs. Blessing is to our souls what light is to our eyes. We need blessing just as our ears need sound waves. Blessings are the substance of life. To ignore blessing is to live life without its fundamental fuel.

Blessing Children

What is particularly important about blessing for our study is that children are specifically mentioned with regard to blessing. Of all the great teachings in the Bible, blessing is one that specifically includes children. The blessing is passed on to children by their parents or another significant person.[2] Blessing is frequently mentioned when God talks to people about giving them children.[3] Often blessing is associated with having children.[4]

---

[2]Genesis 17:18; 24:60; 25:11; 27:4-41; 28:1-4; 31:55; 48:9-20; 49:25-28; 1 Chronicles 16:43; Psalm 37:26; Hebrews 11:20.

[3]Genesis 1:22, 28; 9:1; 17:16, 20; 22:17; 26:3-4, 24; 28:14; 39:5; Psalms 107:38; 112:1-2; 127:5; Proverbs 5:18; Isaiah 51:2; 61:9; 65:23; Luke 1:45; 2:34; 11:27; Acts 3:25; Hebrews 6:14.

[4]Deuteronomy 1:11; 7:13; 28:2-6; 30:19; Joshua 17:14; 1 Chronicles 13:14; Ezekiel 44:30; cf. Luke 23:29.

Blessing comes to those who pay attention to orphans and weak children.[5] God blesses children in Scripture.[6]

Today's children need blessing. The lack of being cherished by significant adults in their lives leaves them lonely, vulnerable, confused, and fearful. Children who have been blessed know they are not alone, that there is a protector, that someone knows the answers and that there is security. Of all the major theological words in the Bible, perhaps blessing has more to do with children than any other.

Blessing is about bringing significant adults into meaningful relationship with children. It involves adults welcoming, nurturing, touching, accepting, listening, teaching, and supporting children. Children were not meant to be alone. They were meant to be favored. They were not to be isolated from human thought and contact, but by the blessing they were made part of the family, part of human history. To pass over the teaching about blessing, or to relegate it to an optional thing that parents can do, or put on the back burner doctrinally, is to remove a significant biblical teaching and to hinder parents and the Christian community in their dealing with children.

Blessing Works

Most children today are lonely. There is no doubt that in our time, in our culture, in our churches, in our families, children plead for adult contact. The biblical paradigm for that contact is blessing. Strikingly, the most extensive treatment of blessing comes in one of the most chaotic events in all of Genesis. Genesis 27 uses the word blessing twenty-two times. It is the

[5]Deuteronomy 24:19; Psalm 41:1; Proverbs 14:21.
[6]Judges 13:24; Job 29:4; Isaiah 44:3.

story of Isaac and Rebekah's disastrous but successful attempt to pass on the blessing to their sons in what seems to be a dysfunctional family. Like most family situations, the story is filled with confusion and actions that we do not understand. We wonder if anything good can come out of this chapter at all. We wonder why the blessing can only be given to one son. We wonder why a blessing once given can't be recalled like a faulty product. We wonder why deception has to play such a role in this chosen family.

Our world reflects the one in Genesis 27. Children in our time grow up in a culture dominated by intrigue, dishonesty, manipulation, and self-centeredness. If the blessing can be passed on through the likes of the chaotic family in Genesis 27, then there is hope that it can be passed on in our troubled society. If Esau can find a blessing from another after being denied the blessing of his father, then there is hope for the blessing-deprived children of our time.

Despite human shortcomings, the blessing works. God's will for the child was done despite the fact that half the family tried to change it and the other half used deceitful means to achieve it. Like Balaam in a later story who is hired to curse, but finds he can only bless, something about the blessing rises above human manipulation and confusion.

Some words of blessing come only indirectly. When God heard Ishmael's cry, he spoke not to the boy but to the mother. Ishmael overheard words of favor:

God heard the boy crying, and the angel of God called to Hagar from heaven and said to her, "What is the mat-

ter, Hagar? Do not be afraid; God has heard the boy crying as he lies there. Lift the boy up and take him by the
hand, for I will make him into a great nation" (Genesis
21:17-18).

Nothing is said about a blessing. Nothing at all is said to
Ishmael. But the words carry concern and protection; they communicate hope and affirmation. Facing certain death, he now
realizes he has a great future.

God the Father sent his son to the earth, yet there is an inti-
mate moment between the two of them when Jesus emerges
from the Jordan River where he has just been baptized by John.
Dripping wet, he looks up to the sky. A dove flies into view and
lands on Jesus. Then come the words. The same God who had
spoken about Ishmael, now speaks to Jesus: "This is my son,
whom I love; with him I am well pleased" (Matthew 3:17).
Matthew doesn't call it a blessing, but it is a significant statement about a son from the father.

Hear the Call

Children need some signal that they are not alone, but
affirmed. Chris Altrock, my co-worker in ministry, tells this
story: "On the Friday before my last birthday, my Dad in New
Mexico e-mailed a short message. It consisted of four sentences.
The third sentence is one of the most significant sentences my
Dad has ever written to me: 'You guys [my brother and me] really make me proud, and I brag on you whenever I get the opportunity.' My Dad is not particularly communicative, so that one

sentence was like an encyclopedia. It made my day. Those six-teen words had a profound impact on me."

Isaac's story, and Jesus' example, encourage us to believe that symbolic actions like touch have amazing power to bless. They challenge us to believe that children who are touched, hugged, kissed, and cuddled will be children who grow up to feel loved, secure, and safe. They challenge us to believe that other symbolic actions like meals together, surprise gifts, and family traditions have a surprising power in the lives of our children.

We may think that a kiss, a meal, laying hands on the head, or placing a child on the knee does not have the same power today that it did in Isaac's day. But it does. In a society that so often practices touching that hurts, that has become so hesitant about any touching at all, there must be a haven where children can be properly and spiritually touched. Because of the confusion about touching in our society, the church must take a clear, powerful, and regular stand against those who abuse children through improper touching. But it must also make a clear, powerful, and regular plea for responsible, godly adults to touch children in godly ways. The church must be a place where godly touching is explained and encouraged and where ungodly abuse is also clearly explained and discouraged. To ignore the godly benefits of touching is to ignore the blessing.

Passing on the Blessing

The blessing baton has been passed to us. Carrying on the work intended in God's ancient promise to Abraham falls to us. Children mean the world to God and they must take on the same significance for us. Just as Jesus blessed children, so we must bless children. As God's people we can either be like Isaac and Rebekah seeking to protect, hoard, and manipulate the blessing or we can be like Jesus, offering the blessing to all who come. As God's people we can either be like the disciples who sought to keep the children away from Jesus, or we can live out the promise that seeks a favor for all.

The doctrine of blessing must be taught in and by the church. It is the church that must proclaim, promote, and practice the passing on of the blessing in our world. It is the church that must teach parents about the blessing. It is the church that must reintroduce the notion of blessing into contemporary thought. It is the church that must reflect on what it means to bless in our culture. It is the church that must insure that God's favor is not forgotten.

Many children never get the blessing from their parents. They grow into adulthood without ever sensing the blessing from those who brought them into the world. Adults who never received the blessing as children struggle to pass it on to their own children. The church must be at their side, offering a delinquent blessing to those blessing-deprived adults and encouraging them to bless the next generation. Adults who never received the blessing as children, yet become parents who pass on the blessing, may be accomplishing one of the greatest achievements of the human race. To be raised without the blessing but become a parent who passes on the blessing is itself a great blessing.

I am convinced that the missing blessing adversely affects children. Without blessing, children seek acceptance, affection, and meaning elsewhere. When the church rises up to champion the blessing of its own children, and the blessing of children in its larger community, they will not only transform the lives of those children, but they will be radically affecting the whole future of their world. When the work of blessing, which is deeply rooted in our biblical faith, is restored to its proper place in our church practice, we will regain the church's most significant tool in helping children. We will lead society in making the world a better place.

Approval Ratings Soar

During that summer of washing bricks and mixing cement, one of the most important events of my life took place. We finished bricking the front of the house. It looked smashing. My father was a perfectionist and there were few professional masons who could match my Dad's finished product. On that last night, we had just cleaned up. The mixer was washed, tools put away, scaffolding taken down, bricks scoured, and it was time to go in for supper. Dad called me aside. He handed me a one dollar bill. He put his hand on my shoulder. He said, "You did a good job."

A good job? Me? The boy who thought he would never amount to anything? Me, the boy who wasn't good at anything? My dad thought I did a good job. The man who had built the perfect wall said that my work was good. He backed it up with money. I've got proof in my pocket. I remember thinking, "I am somebody because somebody important said I did a 'good job.'"

My dad didn't know it, and I certainly didn't know it, but he was doing something that fathers have done since the beginning of time, something deeply biblical, something profoundly godly. He gave me his blessing.

A few years ago I visited a large church in Brooklyn, New York. There were about one thousand people at the early service. The preacher called on an eleven-year-old boy, Joshua Smith, to come to the front. He walked up to the pulpit. The preacher told the church that Joshua had won the sixth grade spelling bee. Then he hugged the boy. What happened next was amazing. The church rose in a standing ovation. They were passing on the blessing.

Churches must be the place where parents find the will and the words to bless their own children. If the home is the nest where the children are raised, the church is the nest where parents are made. Churches must bless parents. Once blessed by the church, parents are more likely to bless their children.

We serve a blessing God. The blessing is a spiritual baton for the human race. God passed it on to us. We must pass it on to those who follow.

Exercises

Hear A Child

1. Tell how the blessing or lack of blessing has affected your life.

2. Share a time you were blessed by a parent or significant adult, or a time you blessed a child.

Hear God's Heart

3. Study the verses about children and blessing. What questions do you have? What conclusions can you draw?

4. Define blessing biblically.

Hear the Call

5. Make a list of children you know or who fall in your sphere of influence. Which ones are receiving the blessing?

6. Discuss ways in which God can use you to bless the children who are not receiving a blessing. Pray for them.

7. List ways the church could teach and influence parents to pass on the blessing.

8. List the repercussions of our failure to bless children.

9. How can we pass on a blessing?
   - from the pulpit
   - in Sunday School
   - in ministries to children
   - in our homes

Chapter Three
God's Answer for Helplessness

Hear A Child

Our congregation's parenting workshop had been on the calendar for months. We advertised widely. A guest expert was coming. That week, after news of the Littleton, Colorado, school shooting reached us, we reexamined our program. We didn't feel we could conduct a parenting workshop in the week after forty-three teenagers were shot in their local high school and not address the issue. Our speaker agreed. We carved an hour out of the seminar time to investigate what we could do.

Our instructor was caught up in the hopelessness of the week just as we were. He told us that we needed to be there for each other. He encouraged us to talk to other people about our anger and fear. We should not be afraid to sit down with our children in order to understand their feelings. He urged us to offer them comfort and to reassure them that they were safe. It was comforting and therapeutic. It helped our grief. But it didn't offer much hope.

> ## ೮೩ ೮೦
> ## These Children
> ## Mean the World
> ## to God
>
> *On December 1, 1997, fourteen year old Michael Carneal took a gun to school in West Paducah, Kentucky, killed three students, and wounded five more. They were praying in a high school hallway. One of the girls who was wounded will be paralyzed from the waist down for the rest of her life. She survived; others did not.*

Few times have I left a church program feeling so powerless. It seemed as though the church had its hands tied behind its back, locked in a remote jail, without a key. Our claim to present a lecture on "How to Stop Violence Against Children" fell on its face. We didn't know the answer. We spent a whole hour proving it. There was no euphoria, no clarity, no direction. Our society was killing its children and there was nothing, nothing at all that we could do. The church had no answers for children.

Bang! Bang! Children Under Fire

Perhaps we were particularly vulnerable to this feeling of helplessness because the school shootings of the late 1990s had encircled us. First came Pearl, Mississippi. That's the little town my family and I go through on the way to the beach each summer. Then came Paducah, Kentucky. One of the girls wounded in the shooting was Melissa Jenkins, who was left paralyzed. Gary Clark organized a group of our teenagers, bought a laptop computer, loaded the kids into the church van and drove to Paducah, found Melissa, and gave her the computer. We felt so helpless. Then Fayetteville, Tennessee. One dead. Our own state.

Pearl to the south. Paducah to the north. Fayetteville to the east. Then came Jonesboro, Arkansas, to the west. Five killed and ten wounded. We listened to one of the teachers tell her story. She had been wounded on the playground. She was the wife of one of the elders at the Bono Church of Christ. People in our congregation had visited that church. We felt helpless.

We Didn't Have Any Answers

When it comes to violence against children and children killing children, who is at fault? Is it the schools or the gun laws or the suburbs or materialism? Is it our pace of life, the lack of school security systems, or substance abuse? Why do we feel so hopeless?

We had no way of explaining what was happening. I did an internet search for what the experts were saying. One helpful site featured the analysis of Dr. Paul Steinhauer. He explained how American children experienced difficulty attaching to significant adults, were unable to meet either excessive or insufficient demands to contain aggression, and failed to deal with loss of ties to extended family, especially when both parents worked outside the home. He argued that violence of children against children and, ultimately, violence of adults against children is due to conflict over changing roles in the family, breakdown of the nuclear

---

[7]Paul D. Steinhauer, M.D., *"Youth in the 80's and 90's–A Fifteen Year Trend: Where Do We Go Next?"* www.voices4children.org/publications/paper-1.htm.

family, a change in the perceived value of mothering, and the transferring of family functions to the community as a whole.[7]

Those points and those of others offered sociological and psychological perspectives, but how do we explain this from a Christian point of view? Are we just to wait helplessly as the Paul Steinhauers tell us why children are dying? Beyond the violence is the more fundamental question of the isolation and confusion felt by today's children. Interviews with students, studies of adolescents, and teenage music all point to the sense of children being ostracized and marginalized. Rejection leads to anger. A few take guns to school, but others pursue drugs, alcohol, sex, or computer games. The issue is not only the violence against and the isolation felt by children, but our own response of hopelessness and despair. Can't we do something beside raising our insurance coverage and praying privately that it doesn't happen to us? Why do we feel so inadequate and paralyzed?

Spiritual Roots of Violence

After our weekend parenting seminar several of us pondered the helplessness and paralysis we all felt at that Sunday night service. Then we realized what had been missing. What about grace? What about the cross of Christ? What about the power of the Word of God to change hearts? What about the God who split the Red Sea and knocked down the walls of Jericho? What about the LORD who changed water to wine and raised the dead? We are not helpless.

There is a solution to violence against children. Our society is caught in the grip of evil. Sin runs unchecked. Someone must identify the problem as sin and direct people to the gospel. Yet the problems faced by children are often excluded from our definition of gospel. Christians often see no link between children and the gospel, but the two are intertwined. The gospel is about sin and grace. The problems facing children today are spiritual and the response should be a spiritual one.

The more we try to reduce problems of children to science or education and the more we seek an answer from the humanistic world, the more deeply our children get mired in the problem. Science and materialism created the problem by leaving spiritual values at the door. Only the gospel offers a workable solution. The Bible explores the spiritual option on its opening pages.

Hear God's Heart

The Bible begins with violence of child against child and of adults against children. Within the first four chapters of Genesis one brother kills another and then a grown man kills a child. We might imagine what it was like to be the first parents and get the news of bloodshed in the field.

"I'm sorry to have to tell you this, but I bear bad news." Eve steadied herself. Adam began to perspire.

"I am sorry, but your son Abel has been murdered." Gasp. Silence. Sobs.

"Please excuse me, but I'm afraid I have more bad news. Your older son Cain is under investigation for the murder."

Perhaps they expected it. Rivalry between their two sons began when God rejected Cain's sacrifice. Then the report came that they were fighting in the field. Now the word that their baby was dead. Nobody knows how old Cain and Abel were. Cain survived the ordeal and later had a child, but it seems that they were both single when they approached the altar. Let's say Cain was eighteen and Abel sixteen. They were the first children.

The story of Eve's loss of her son comes in the middle of the Bible's opening pages with descriptions of creation, the beginning of humanity, the great flood and the tower of Babel. Two themes dominate this material in Genesis 1-11, the spread of sin and the corresponding spread of grace.

Sin begins in the garden. Adam and Eve eat of the tree of the knowledge of good and evil. Cain kills Abel. Lamech murders another man and then a child. The sons of God mate with the daughters of men. Finally, the spread of human sin reaches so far "that every imagination of the thoughts of his heart was only evil continually" (Genesis 6:5). After the flood there was a sin in Noah's tent and in the tower-builder's pride.

But alongside this terrible stain is a corresponding spread of grace. Adam and Eve are told if they eat they will die, but they don't die. Cain doesn't go to prison. He gets a mark. Humanity is destroyed by a flood, but a boat saves eight people. After the flood the rainbow becomes a symbol of grace. The pride of the tower builders is quickly followed by the blessing to Abraham. As sin spread, so did grace.

The Bible is specific about the first sins: (1) Adam and Eve eat of the tree of the knowledge of good and evil. (2) Cain kills Abel. (3) Lamech kills a man. (4) Lamech kills a child. It's hard to miss it. When the Bible starts to define sin, it first mentions hurting children. Two of the first four sins involve violence against children. The first sin in the home is the violence between brothers. It took only five generations (Adam to Lamech) for an adult to abuse a child.

Violence against children is not new. We may hear more about it. More children may be abused in our time than in theirs, but hurting children is not new. Before school shootings and abusive mothers, before wicked men kidnaped children and wars injured five-year-olds, long before all that, Abel's blood flowed into the fresh soil outside the garden and a nameless child killed by Lamech was carried to his grave.

Behind all the abuse and hurting of children is one thing: sin. Behind every uncle or aunt who abuses a niece and all the dead children in war-torn lands, behind all the school shootings and crack cocaine babies, behind it all is sin. All have sinned and fallen short of the glory of God. The same thing that happened in Genesis 4 continues to happen. Brother killing brother. Children being abused. The problem in Genesis 4 was sin. The problem today is sin.

The opening pages of Genesis set up all that follows. Sin is the fundamental problem. Sin affects children in negative ways. Where there is sin, grace soon follows. What we have in Genesis is the beginning of the gospel. The grace God showed in Genesis 1-11 finds its ultimate expression in Jesus. When Jesus died on the cross he gave us power over sin. The sin he gave us power over includes violence. The gospel is the power of God for salvation from the wickedness of violence, and from the pain of violence against children.

Hear the Call

Genesis 1-11 reminds us that the ongoing tension between sin and grace involves children. Children meant so much to God that he introduced grace and eventually supplied the gospel as the means of protecting and saving children. The church too often separates the sins of violence against children from the saving gospel of Jesus. We too often despair over the abuse of children, never even thinking of the gospel as the most biblical and most powerful response.

Blessing and gospel are two biblical doctrines that relate directly to children. Gospel relates directly to children because most people respond to the gospel as children. Surveys reveal that most of the members of most churches became Christians as young people. Gospel relates directly to violence against children, because it is the fundamental means Christians have of changing the world. Violence is sin and sin can only be removed by the grace of God.

What About Eddie?

In the late 1950s a Nashville minister, Ira North, brought ten-year-old Eddie into his Madison pulpit one Sunday morning. He asked Eddie if he had ever been to a Church of Christ before. "No, sir." Ira told him that the church loved everybody and they loved him. "Eddie, you're as welcome here as the President of the United States." After North sent Eddie out, he told the church about his conversation with the juvenile court judge. Eddie's crime was that he was unloved, unwanted, and uncared for.

"Brother North," the judge said, "I'm going to have to send Eddie to reform school just to get him off the street. Nobody gives a hoot about Eddie."

Then North looked into the eyes of his congregation as he said, "As you get in your big fancy cars and go to your big fancy houses where you have your fancy clothes, I want you to think about Eddie. I'm not against nice cars, big houses, or fancy clothes, but what about Eddie?"

Ira North took a critical step that day when he walked into the Madison pulpit with a child in tow. He made Eddie a gospel issue. The same gospel which told people that God so loved the world that he gave us his only son also included Eddie. By bringing this unwanted child to the place where the gospel was preached, North in a visual way was widening his congregation's understanding of the gospel. He was putting the gospel back into its foundational perspective.

As North preached, Madison member Perry Underwood leaned over to talk to his wife. Then in the middle of the sermon, he jumped to his feet.

"Hold on, Brother North, Eddie has a home," Underwood declared. "We'll take him until you build a children's home."

That was the beginning of a church that re-linked the gospel with children. They started caring for children on the church property. Women of the church made clothing for poor children. Ira North knew the gospel was linked with children.

But more than one church benefitted from that story. North talked about Eddie and Perry Underwood all across the nation. Other congregations listened and poured themselves into children and helping the poor. The story of what happened at Madison reminded them of the one who emptied himself at the cross.

The Gospel Includes Children

North realized that the church had marginalized children. Their rejection and disaffection were due to widespread adult selfishness and self-centeredness. Children were growing up without the blessing. Adults expected children to give up childhood and become adults as quickly as possible. The church lobby had become a place to complain about paying taxes for school systems. Children's Sunday School and Youth Ministry were seen as ways to babysit the children while the adults did the real spiritual work. Eddie changed all that. North reminded the church that the gospel had the power to deal with the Eddies of the world.

Those who promote sin are everywhere. There is no shortage of those following the pattern in Genesis 1-11 to bring about an increase in sin. The promotion of sin never runs low on fuel, it never has a shortage of supporters, it never stops its endless campaign to ruin the race.

But sin is not unopposed. Grace can conquer sin. God showed grace when he made fig-leaf clothes for Adam and Eve, continued it when he rescued the "children of Israel" out of Egyptian bondage, and brought it to a grand crescendo when he made us sons and daughters by the death of his son on the cross. So much of the redemptive story, from younger brother Abel to the son dying on the cross, is told through the vocabulary of children. Yet too often, children have been removed from the gospel. Theology is about adults. Children must be hushed and held in waiting until they can be adults.

Then Ira North brought Eddie to the pulpit. "I'm not against nice cars, big houses, or fancy clothes, but what about Eddie?"

Hurting Children Must Benefit from the Gospel

I am calling for a change in how we look at children in the church and in the world. We must not see the problems of the world's children separate from the gospel. The sinful world wreaks havoc with children. The gospel is their only hope. Only God can conquer sin. We must not allow culture to shut out the gospel message. We must not retreat. We must not be so concerned with internal issues that the dying, hurting, endangered children of the world receive none of the gospel's power because we keep it bottled up inside our churches. Hurting children in every community must benefit from the gospel.

We must include children in the way we look at church. From budgeting to bulletins, from elders' meetings to activities for senior citizens, from Sunday morning services to hiring new staff, children must be considered part of the focus of how we do church. We must keep an Eddie near the pulpit to remind us that the gospel includes children. Church funds should be spent to insure that the children inside our churches and the ones outside our buildings know about the gospel. The church is not a place to isolate us from the cries of hurting children, but a center from which God sends out rescue teams.[8]

Different institutions make up our society. Government makes laws against hurting children. Education provides materials to train us to live together in harmony. Industry makes

---

[8]How the church ministers to children is the focus of this book. The next five chapters will look at ways in which the local church must include children in the gospel.

products to protect children. Medicine finds ways to repair the damage violence does to children.

But none of those institutions deals with the real issue. Governments pass laws, but they cannot change hearts. Education provides insight, but it can't remake the soul. Industry offers a better product, but it will not change character. Medicine repairs the physical heart, but it cannot repair the spiritual heart. Only one institution in society is charged with telling people about sin and the cross. Only one institution in society is prepared to deal with the fundamental issues causing violence to children. Only the church can point the way to change human hearts.

When we use the gospel which is at the core of our biblical faith as the lens through which we view children and the focus by which we minister to children, we restore the gospel's power to our work with children. When we seek out the lonely and hurting children of our world with the gospel, we will bring about a transformation in the life of each child we reach. And by that changed child God will be well on his way to changing other parts of our sinful world.

We should not be paralyzed when we hear of school shootings. Society in Genesis 1-11 engaged in spiritual warfare between the expanding forces of sin and the growing cavalry of grace. Problems in our society have the same spiritual roots. We are not paralyzed. We are not helpless. We are not in a remote jail with our hands tied behind our backs. We are conduits for the power of God. Scripture gives us a theological framework by which we understand the evil of our age. Violence of children against children and violence of adults against children is rooted in a fallen humanity. The solution is found in a risen LORD. Like Ira North we must bring the children to our pulpit and ask today's Christians, "What about Eddie?"

What Will Your Church Do with Eddie?

In April 1997, I called three people to the front of our Family Life Center at our congregation in Memphis. It didn't occur to me then, but we were doing exactly the same thing in our congregation that North had done at Madison. We were making the problems faced by children a gospel issue.

One was ten-year-old Levi Dillard. That day he committed his life to Christ. What he did was not cute or sentimental, it was gospel. He left a life of sin and embraced the gift of grace. He was baptized minutes later.

Then there was Kenny White, who had just been honored in Memphis as First Tennessee Bank's Adult Volunteer of the Year. He had organized an aluminum can recycling effort at the bank's branches, collected three tons of recycled metal, and raised three thousand dollars, which the bank donated to our congregation's school store, an annual effort to provide poor children with school supplies. Because of people like Kenny, every year over five thousand disadvantaged children receive all the pencils and paper they need.

Kenny's presence at the front was significant because of the way our congregation had embraced the school store. For us it was a gospel issue. The store was a statement to the larger Memphis community that children are important to God, that we are not powerless to deal with the issues they face. In a sense

Kenny brought the souls of the five thousand disadvantaged school children to the place where the gospel was proclaimed.

The third person was a grandmother, Betty Dollar. She quit her real estate job, sold her house, and moved to Ukraine, where she now works morning until night teaching the Bible to children and visiting orphans. In that city, a new church was taking root. In a world where we often feel powerless, this grandmother represented the power of the gospel in action. The lives of dozens of children were being touched. People were bowing at the foot of the cross through the power of the gospel she carried.

There I stood, with three great servants of God. I felt a bit like Ira North must have felt when he brought Eddie to the front of the Madison church. That's where children belong. Children are a gospel issue. We are not alone. We need not be paralyzed.

After I introduced them, I realized we didn't have a plan for leaving the platform. The four of us stood there a bit awkwardly. But as Levi, Kenny, and Betty wondered what to do next, standing with me in front of the congregation, we were all surprised. A wonderful thing happened. A few people started to applaud, just a sprinkling here and there, and then a deafening roar, and they rose to their feet in unison. For five loud minutes, they celebrated the gospel and children.

Exercises

Hear A Child

1. Tell about a child you know who has been ill-treated.

2. Give an example of a time when you felt powerless to help a child.

Hear God's Heart

3. Discuss the violence done to children in the Bible. Study cases in the list below:

    ♦   In Genesis 4:23 Lamech says, "I have killed a man for wounding me. A young man for injuring me." The word for young man is actually child. Lamech killed a child.

    ♦   Lot offered his two daughters to the wicked men of the city (Genesis 19:8).

    ♦   Abraham sent his oldest son to the desert (Genesis 21:14).

    ♦   Pharaoh ordered the Hebrew midwives to let the boy babies die (Exodus 1:16).

    ♦   Job's children were killed in a violent storm (Job 1:18-19).

    ♦   Jephthah came home and killed his virgin teenage daughter because of a vow he made (Judges 11:34-35).

    ♦   The Ephramite from Gibeah offered his virgin daughter to the sexually charged men of the city (Judges 19:24).

    ♦   Two harlots brought two babies, one dead, one alive to Solomon so he could tell them which one belonged to which mother. Solomon called for a sword to cut the living baby in half (1 Kings 3:16-28).

    ♦   The evil queen Athaliah tried to kill the boy king, Joash, but his aunt hid him (2 Kings 11:1-3).

- Ahaz burned his son as an offering (2 Kings 16:3).

- Other Judean kings burned their sons and daughters in the Valley of Hinnom (Jeremiah 7:31).

- In the 8th century B.C., Judean landowners abused the children of the poor (Micah 2:9).

- During the fall of Jerusalem to the Babylonians, hungry mothers ate their own children, and dead children were piled in the streets (Lamentations 2:20-21).

- When King Herod heard about the birth of Jesus, he ordered his soldiers to Bethlehem to kill all the boy children under the age of two years (Matthew 2:16).

- Jesus anticipated a severe future in which fathers would slay their own sons (Mark 13:12).

Hear the Call

4. Discuss what you hear in public prayers in your congregation about children. Discuss how things could be different.

5. List ways in which children in your community are subjected to violence. Why does your church pray or not pray about these issues?

6. Describe your reactions to the response of the Madison Church to what Ira North did that Sunday.

7. What would your church do with an Eddie?

8. How has your church linked the gospel with children?

9. Ask to look at your church budget. Does it include children (inside and outside the church) hearing the gospel? Discuss possible changes, if needed, to include children.

Chapter Four
God Guides Children

Hear A Child

As a young minister I was part of a team sent to plant a new church in Milwaukee, Wisconsin. Our training emphasized evangelism. Sent out to save souls, our success would be measured by how many were won. That principle drove all that we did. It was our method and our goal. Since we were a new church, we had to save souls or fail.

Two years after starting the new congregation in 1977, we moved into our own building. In our new facility no group moved more than the babies. The nursery was originally off the main hallway. Then the church grew and we had to remodel. We needed part of the nursery for a coat rack, so the infants were relocated. Then we expanded the auditorium. The baby nursery was in the way, so the cribs traveled again. Then we put on an addition. The babies made another move.

The Kids are in the Way

The constant movement of the nursery created tension between Joyce, who advocated for good child care, and me, one of the ministers. She had in mind a ministry to children. I had in mind a ministry to adults where we could save souls. She saw children as an end. I saw them as a means to an end. My operative principle was "save souls of adults." She operated on "do what's best for the children." So we clashed. And the nursery moved.

Moving the nursery to a new room typified my theology which had no room for children. Despite my own conversion through Vacation Bible School, as a minister of the church I was not a great advocate for VBS. It drained away too many resources that could be used to win adults. In my view children were a problem to be handled, not a ministry to be accomplished. Children were not to be seen and not heard. Out of sight and out of mind. So we kept moving the nursery to make room for adults.

My resistance to ministering to children had begun in college when I worked as part of an inner city ministry. Helping poor kids attracted many college students to the center city where families lived in cardboard houses, uncared-for children came to church in nothing but T-shirts during the winter months, and it was easy to fill up a classroom in the cement block mission building with dirty ten-year-olds. My friends found the ministry attractive because it gave them a sense of purpose. They were rocks of stability in the lives of children awash in a sea of poverty and confusion. They loved arriving at church with three or four kids hanging on their necks. Sharing their meager resources with children who had even less made them feel like they made a difference.

What I saw was confusion. The chaotic lives the children lived in their run-down houses with their dysfunctional parents were mirrored in the chaotic Bible classes taught off-the-cuff by unprepared college students, and services that were noisy, unfocused, and unplanned. What I saw was not attractive. I didn't work in that ministry long, but what I concluded from that effort, unfortunately, stayed in my thinking for years.

If this project had a clearly thought-out theology of ministry or a plan for service, it never made it to most of us college students. We had a strong desire, but not much of a plan. I concluded that because that ministry was chaotic, all ministry to children had no place in the church. It never occurred to me that there might be a scriptural demand that we serve children. I came to believe that we took care of children in order to do real ministry among adults.

Where Do Children Fit in Church?

How do we think about children as a church? Are they just adults in waiting? Are children incomplete humans that must be shuffled off to other rooms until they are ready for "big church?" Do we pursue ministries to children because we have thought seriously about what the Bible says about children or because adults demand that their young be taken care of while the grownups attend to God's business? How do we evaluate whether or not our children's ministries are effective or biblical? Do we as a church provide a place for children to be nurtured? Do we have a theological understanding of why we provide that nurture?

A couple of years ago I began searching for a book that explained a biblical view of children, or gave a theological foundation for ministering to children. Some attempts do exist, but none satisfied me because they mostly quoted texts that mentioned children as if to say, "See, children are mentioned in the Bible" and then went on to explain the intellectual development of children, offering clear insights from the fields of education, psychology, and sociology. I learned about *how* we can help children develop, but found little about the theological significance of *why* we did it.

Hear God's Heart

As we minister to children, there is no better model than Jesus himself. Several times in the gospels he turns to children. What he does with them, how he responds to them, and how he regards them is instructive as we construct a theology behind our own ministry to children.

In Mark 10:13-16 Jesus talks about children and, in the process, gives us a definition of childhood and leaves a challenge for the contemporary church. The brief incident involving Jesus and the children also appears in Matthew 19:13-15 and Luke 18:15-17. Some unnamed people were bringing children to Jesus. Many speculate on who these people were. In Mark and Luke the encounter is preceded by Jesus' teaching on marriage and divorce, leading some to suggest that these children were from divorced homes being brought to Jesus by surrogate parents. The text does not say. These unnamed individuals wanted Jesus to touch the little ones. But they couldn't get close enough. They ran into a circle of disciples, poised like Secret Service agents around Jesus, protecting him from on-comers. Jesus was indignant. It's one of the few times in the gospels when Jesus became angry. We might imagine that with an intense frown on his face he clenched his fist and raised his voice.

LET THE LITTLE CHILDREN COME TO ME!

The disciples had misunderstood Jesus. They thought their view of children was the same as his. There should be no children here, the disciples believed. In many ways their view of children parallels the stance I took in Milwaukee: keep the children at a distance so we can get "real ministry" done. But Jesus' response to their attempt to keep the children away from him leads us in a different direction. I believe we have, in what Jesus *says*, the foundation for a theology of ministering to children. This chapter is not based on Jesus *welcoming the children*, which is a wonderful model for the church to follow (see chapter 7), nor on his *blessing of the children*, which is a continuation of a fundamental biblical doctrine about children (see chapter 2), but this argument is based on *what he says*: "I tell you the truth, anyone who will not receive the kingdom of God like a little child will never enter it" (Mark 10:15).

What Would Jesus Say?

Jesus implies in this text that children are moldable, teachable and in the process of formation. That insight will go on to provide biblical guidance for how we minister to children. If they are moldable and teachable and in the process of becoming, our response to them must be not just to have activities, but to mold; not just to babysit, but to teach; not to rush them into adulthood, but to let them move steadily through childhood. My argument has three stages: (1) explaining the phrase "the kingdom of God," (2) exploring what Jesus means by "be like children," and (3) drawing out Jesus' underlying understanding of what it means to be a child.

The Kingdom of God. After the seemingly simultaneous rebuke and welcome, Jesus explains his actions. The kingdom of God belongs to such as these. Jesus used big words in the presence of the little ones. "Kingdom of God" carried heavy theological freight in both the Old and New Testaments. While the phrase is used nearly seventy times, the concept appears more frequently. It is what God wants done. It is the rule of God on earth. When Jesus talks about the kingdom of God he is speaking about something central. In his model prayer he would say, "Your kingdom come, your will be done." Same point.

This ceases to be a cute outing Jesus has with children when he uses the words "kingdom of God." He is bringing in central biblical concepts. He is making pronouncements about what God wants, about how we are to live, about his mission. He finds one quality of children that reminds him of this kingdom, something about children that all of us should imitate.

"Be like little children." The kingdom of God does not belong *to* children, but to those who become *like* children. Children are an example, they are a visual aid, of what it takes to be in the kingdom, to be supportive of God's plan for the world, to be in sync with the Father. Jesus then explains further, "anyone who will not receive the kingdom of God like a little child will never enter it" (Mark 10:15). Jesus uses children to illustrate the kingdom, to show what God wants in the world. They are not the kingdom, but those who capture the central qualities of children will be in the kingdom.

What does it mean to be "like a child?" Children have many qualities. They can be immature, dirty, noisy, bothersome, expensive, sickly, irresponsible, demanding, and prideful. Children are often naughty and insolent. Jesus was aware of the pettiness of children in Luke 7:32 when he quotes them singing, "We played the flute for you, and you did not dance; we sang a dirge, and you did not cry." It's the ancient version of "we asked you and you didn't want to play with us." No child is perfect. No child is an ideal little angel all of the time. To suggest that Jesus speaks of any of these qualities runs counter to the whole gospel message.

ଔ ଈ

This Child Means the World to God

Timmy grew up in a public housing project. His mother worked hard to hold the family together, but could not provide all the things the children needed. One summer she sent Timmy to a local church for Vacation Bible School. Timmy didn't have shoes, and it didn't seem to matter since it was summertime, but the people at the church stopped him at the door. They would not teach children without shoes.

When Jesus called adults to be like children, he meant to be moldable and open like children. Luke's account of Jesus and the children falls between two events that have similar themes. In Luke 18:9-14 Jesus contrasts a Pharisee who prays a prideful prayer of self-sufficiency with a publican who won't even look to heaven but confesses his dependence and lowly status. After the account of the children all three synoptic gospels record the approach of the rich young ruler, self-confident, self-sufficient, and independent. Around him stand the disciples who have humbly given up family and fortune to follow Jesus. In the middle is the call to be like children, moldable like the publican who knows his limits, and open like the disciples who have committed all to Jesus.

In Mark 10:24 Jesus says, "Children, how hard it is to enter the kingdom of God!" Jesus' use of the word "children" in referring to adults recalls his encounter with those who were literally children, reminding them that they must be willing like a child to enter the kingdom. The childlike qualities Jesus seeks to imitate are those associated with the dependent status of children.

The dependence of children is reflected in the first beatitude: "Blessed are the poor in spirit for theirs is the kingdom of heaven" (Matthew 5:3). Jesus' teaching about discipleship begins with "deny yourself" (Luke 9:23). Children by nature are poor in spirit. They are naturally dependent. Their souls are in the process of being formed and molded.

Jesus gives us a theology of entering the kingdom, but at the same time he gives us a critical insight into children. Just as becoming children of God means openness to God's work in *our* lives, so being human children means openness to God's work in *their* lives.

Jesus' Understanding of Childhood. Jesus understood what it means to be a child. Being a child means to be moldable, easily changed. A child is teachable, entering the world unformed. Childhood is a process of formation, of being incomplete. Children are dependent, unable to provide for themselves. Children are innocent of the adult world's evil, unscarred by sin.

In a striking way Jesus makes a case for children to be children. His point to the adults depends on each human going through a stage called childhood in which they are open to being formed and molded. Those in the kingdom must take on that quality of children. Jesus recognized that childhood was a needed and critical part of life in which children are led and guided into adulthood. That part of human development must be recaptured by each adult to enter the kingdom of God.

Hear the Call

This understanding of children leads to two aspects of our ministry to children. (1) Children are moldable and must be taught. (2) The church must call for children to be allowed to experience childhood.

Children are Moldable and Must Be Taught

Programs such as Sunday school, Vacation Bible School, and Christian camp are often thought to be conveniences for parents in the congregation. But there is a clear biblical reason for such programs. These kinds of ministries to children are clearly the church teaching children, providing a place for them, allowing them to be molded by the gospel. By these ministries churches recognize that children must experience childhood: they must be taught, led, and provided for until they reach adulthood. As the church teaches, shows mercy, evangelizes, and worships, it must provide a way for children to be part of those church functions.

Each Christian must be careful not to imitate the disciples. The disciples kept children away from Jesus for some reason. Children can be bothersome and time-consuming. Any situation involving children calls for adjustments by adults. Ministries among children are volunteer-intensive. Providing a safe and clean nursery or operating classes for preschool and elementary-aged children takes patience and effort. Being a church that molds and mentors teenagers requires many hours of dedicated labor. Clearly none of these ministries are specifically indicated in the Bible, just as pews, communion ware, zones, and adult Bible classes are not mentioned, but they are wonderful tools to allow each Christian to have the same view of children that Jesus did.

Infants are teachable. They learn to eat and smile. Soon they learn to walk and talk. Adults and parents guide them in these things. Children do not make decisions independently about whether they are going to eat, smile, walk, or talk. They learn as they are guided. Learning about spiritual things takes the same path. They are guided from an early age to learn about God and to understand Jesus.

Luke 18:15 says, "People were also bringing babies to Jesus. . . ." As followers of Jesus we continue to call the children to come to Jesus. Such a calling may simply be a safe nursery where children are held. The call is clearly the rationale behind children's Bible classes where each child is permitted to learn as a child, where instruction can be directed in a way they can understand. Youth ministry is a call for teenagers to come to Jesus, seeking to connect with young people in years of major decision-making. Children do not come into the world as believers. They must be taught, molded, led, and given the chance to form faith of their own. Children do not come with a complete sense of morality, but they must be informed and shown what is good and right.

At some point each child must make a decision about God and conversion to Christ. The Bible is silent on the conversion of children. Those converted in the New Testament were those who had come to faith in Jesus and recognized their own sinfulness before God. No one was saved against their will. No one was baptized without first hearing the word of God taught. All of that suggests that children must be carefully taught and led toward conversion. Parents, teachers, and mentors must walk with them and guide them.

The Future of the Church

Children must be taught about God and led to faith. Their relationship with God must be thought through by those who guide the church's ministry to children and prayerfully considered by those who teach in the Sunday school. Guiding a roomful of children to know God is one of the most challenging tasks in the entire church. Current statistics show that almost half of the children raised in church leave it as adults.[9] This sobering fact drives us back to the Sunday school classroom and our perspective on children. Churches which place unprepared teach-

---

[9]David K. Lewis, Carley H. Dodd, and Darryl L. Tippens, *The Gospel According to Generation X* (Abilene, TX: ACU Press, 1995), p vii.

ers in front of impressionable youngsters, Sunday school teachers who view their task as babysitting rather than leading young minds to faith, and congregations where so little emphasis is placed on children that workers in that ministry are difficult to recruit must be reevaluated in light of the gospel story. Preachers and elders who ignore ministry to children, services which never acknowledge the children present, congregations which never pray that their own children will come to faith are like the disciples who kept the children away from Jesus. Sunday school literature, videos of Bible stories, puppet stages with bright lights and funny characters, elaborate Vacation Bible School productions, and state-of-the-art classrooms all contribute to leading children to God. But these strategies cannot replace the spiritual role of adults who have the same mind about children that Jesus did.

Nothing may be more critical for tomorrow's church than what is happening in the preschool through high school classrooms today. It may not be apparent for fifteen years, but the emphasis a church places on molding its own children will be crucial in the days to come. Nothing may be more critical to the church's immediate future than the work under the guidance of the youth minister. Repeated surveys of current church members show that more than ninety percent came to faith as teens. There is no more fertile evangelistic field than the junior and senior high classes. There is no larger group in any church seeking answers than the teen group. Any church that allows its ministry to teens to be reduced to ski trips and nights at the skating rink is following in the footsteps of the disciples who kept the children away from Jesus.

The Gospel and Children

At a church staff meeting one day we talked about how non-Christian teenagers visiting our church would hear about the gospel. Later my fellow staff member Buster Clemens and I met further to pray and discuss the matter. It was a remarkable discussion. I'll never forget it. It was so clear, so obvious, so evident. We insist on an invitation in each worship service. It is a time when the gospel is presented and people are urged to respond. Why don't we do that in Sunday school? How could we insist that the invitation be offered in every worship service, but in the places where we taught the Bible we seldom explained the gospel? We asked our church to join us in making a commitment that in every gathering of the church we would tell people about the gospel.

Buster coaches a junior high football team. That night was the awards banquet. As part of his speech, he urged his junior high football players to consider Jesus. He told them he was open to talking with them, that he was concerned about more than developing their tackling or blocking skills. He wanted them to be fully prepared to meet life.

Children are growing up all around us. Whether that teachable, impressionable mind hears about Jesus is up to us. We do not want to miss an opportunity to carry on this important ministry. I no longer believe the nursery is a room that must be moved to do adult ministry. The church must make sure it allows and helps the children to come to Jesus.

A Place for Children to Be Children

The first part of a ministry to children leads to a second. The church must provide a place for children to be children and must call society to the same task. Children must not be rushed through childhood either by society or by the church.

The church's role in caring for children comes at a critical time in our culture's attitude toward children. Increasingly, children in our society are pressed into adult situations. Bookstore shelves reflect this trend in American society. Neil Postman's *The Disappearance of Childhood* and Marie Winn's *Children Without Childhood* head the list. David Elkind called his book *The Hurried Child*. Alex Kotlowitz was more direct with his *There Are No Children Here*. They all take up the same issue: American culture tends to deny childhood.

James Dobson talked with a sixth-grade teacher in a middle-class California city. She asked her class to complete the sentence, "I wish. . . ." Twenty of her thirty students made reference to their troubled home life:

"I wish my parents wouldn't fight and I wish my father would come back."

"I wish my mother didn't have a boyfriend."

"I wish I could get straight A's so my father would love me."

"I wish I had one mom and one dad so the kids wouldn't make fun of me."

"I wish I had an M-1 rifle so I could shoot those who make fun of me."[10]

---

[10]James Dobson, *Love Must Be Tough* (Waco: Word, 1983), p 3.

When Jesus said "anyone who will not receive the kingdom of God like a little child" he did not have in mind the kind of childhood Dobson describes. He had in mind children who were permitted to be lowly and dependent and humble and teachable, not those exposed to adult sins and adult responsibilities.

What Would Jesus Do?

After rebuking the disciples for turning the children away and after urging the adult crowd to imitate the dependence of childhood, Jesus then models what he expects from all people. He does what we should do. He shows how to treat children. He cuddles them and blesses them. The childhood that Jesus respects is what many children today are denied. Some adults, instead of seeking to be like children to gain access to the kingdom, give up that childlike status themselves and force physical children to give it up, also. In too many homes and in too many churches we say, "There are no children here. Hurry up, child, it's time to be an adult."

While we live in a culture that tends to strip childhood away from children, there are many who dedicate themselves to helping children be children. Medical people trained in pediatrics, counselors who specialize in childhood therapy, educators who take a degree in elementary or secondary education, and adults who work in child care are among those who recognize the need to protect, advocate for, and guide children. People in these occupations are members of almost all congregations. Their daily work has a direct link to Jesus' concern with children. In a sense they are part of one of God's largest army of workers, those who care for children. Not supported by the church for the most part, their occupations permit them to do for children what Jesus did for children. Their secular occupations take on a distinctly spiritual aspect. The local school system or insurance claims may pay their salary, but in one clear sense they work for God.

Many churches find it beneficial to pray for those who work among children in their community. As they model joy, kindness, love, mercy, patience, and other Christian attributes among children, they have a mighty influence in a dark world. Some churches encourage members engaged in occupations linked with children to promote good moral principles among children, and urge these workers to pray daily for the children they serve. A few congregations have invited others from the community to come to special services where the entire church shows its support for those who work among children. Others have placed books in local libraries that promote the safety, advocacy, and guidance of children.

The Challenge

As the adult leaders of churches, we too often place concerns at the center of the congregation's agenda that neglect children or consider the work among children as insignificant. We often join the larger culture in rushing children into adulthood. But caring for children as children is deeply rooted in the ministry of our Lord and anchored at the core of our faith. Children do mean the world to God. When churches refocus on their own children in a biblical way and realize their spiritual obligation to the children around them, then we restore God's intention of hearing the cries of lonely and confused children and being conduits to transform their lives. When we change a child we also radically alter the future. By changing children we transform the world.

Let the Children Come

I regret the leadership decisions I made in the church that neglected children. I'm grateful for women like Joyce in Milwaukee and others who led me to see the concerns of Jesus. Now several times a year in our congregation we dedicate a service to children. In my lessons I regularly mention Sunday school teachers, nursery workers, and others who minister to the young. These ministries are the most important in our congregation. I believe that. I teach that. We think of ourselves as a church for children.

Suppose the simple events of Jesus' encounter with the children happened in your church. What role would you have played? The disciples thought they were following Jesus by keeping the children away. They were wrong. Will you let the children come?

Exercises

Hear A Child

1. What childhood memories do you have of being in church? Was your experience positive or negative? Why?

2. Describe a time in your childhood when you were pushed into an adult situation.

3. Describe a child you know who is being forced into an adult situation.

Hear God's Heart

4. Who do you think brought the children to Jesus?

5. Why do you think the disciples turned the children away?

6. Is your personal attitude toward children more like Jesus or the disciples? Give examples.

7. Jesus tells us to become like children. Give examples of attitudes and actions you've observed in children that you want to imitate.

Hear the Call

8. How can churches protect children from sin?

9. Discuss ways in which part of the congregation's mission can be the salvation of its own biological children.

10. Make a list of people who work with children in your community. Make copies for church leaders and ask them to pray for those on the list.

Chapter Five
Helping Families Survive

Hear A Child

Think for a moment about the Jensens, a family in our congregation. Look at them from the point of view of their oldest daughter, Mandy. Every week day she leaves for school at 7:30 A.M. and is back home at 3:00 P.M. Mandy has nightly homework. Her friends come over every few weekends for a sleep over. Saturdays are split between cub sports and ballet classes. Activities at church take up most of Sunday except when her cub sports soccer games are scheduled during the afternoon. After Sunday morning at church and Sunday afternoon at soccer, the whole family stays home at night in near exhaustion.

For three years she has had ballet class on Saturdays. Several times a year they have special programs. One weekend her ballet class performed a Saturday morning program in town and another program on Sunday afternoon at a school 90 miles away.

The Church-Going Family

On top of all this activity, her Sunday school class has regular events outside of Sunday morning. The children participate in three or four major programs during the year. Mandy's Sunday school teachers stress the importance of the entire class being at these events. The Jensens pray at meal times, but there is seldom time for any other spiritual activities at home. Each child has his own Bible. The whole family attends church and Sunday school each week.

Mandy feels pressure from school to participate in extracurricular activities. Mandy's friends urge her to do everything, buy everything, be everything, and go to everything. She pleads with her parents to let her be like her friends. Mandy likes to read the advertisements in the Sunday paper and often asks her parents to buy her what she sees.

Mandy's parents juggle their schedule with caring for Mandy's invalid grandmother who lives with them. Mandy has a younger sister and brother who are not yet in school. Her five-year-old sister and two-year-old brother spend Monday through Friday at day care. Both of her parents have jobs outside the home. Mandy has never heard a family discussion about why both of her parents work. Family finances are strained even with both parents employed.

Mandy worries about her cousins who used to go to the same congregation. Mrs. Jensen and her sister both grew up at the church where the Jensens now attend. Several years ago Mrs. Jensen's married sister was divorced. Mandy's aunt no longer attends church. Her cousins never see their father. The issue is spoken about in hushed tones.

The family runs from one thing to another. The Jensens feel harassed, like they are fighting the ocean waves without a boat. The parents feel guilty if they do not attend Mandy's every activity. When the entire family is at home, they often go to their separate rooms where they watch television or where the children play video games. Sometimes Mandy hears her parents fighting about family matters.

Mandy is eleven.

Job Description

The adult Jensens have become chauffeurs, umpires, assistant coaches, sponsors, cake bakers, appointment keepers, graduation organizers, fashion consultants, computer programmers, telephone operators, message takers, internet censors, movie reviewers, room mothers, audiences, cheerleaders, emergency medical technicians, Sunday school teachers, nurses, bus drivers, fund raisers, contributors, magazine buyers, costume makers, banquet planners, poster makers, and, occasionally, parents.

The Jensens are a real family, typical of how many Americans live. They are also a Christian family where church is a central part of their lives. But their lifestyle raises questions. Who speaks for kids so busy with life that they seldom see their parents? What is the changing role of the family doing to the isolation that children feel? Where are the issues facing the family discussed? Where do families get direction? Who encourages families to nurture a life rather than just negotiate a schedule? Who helps mothers to mother rather than just provide transportation? Who directs dads to be more than a source of funding?

I Am Concerned

Of all the issues raised in this book, I feel most unprepared to discuss this one. I feel the same pressures as the Jensen family. If there is any place where I feel frustrated, it is in speaking up for children who are growing up in frenzied, unfocused, harassed families. I see children being penalized in our church family because they come from single-parent family homes. I hear young children cry out because they are being pressured by parents, teachers and coaches to excel beyond their time and abilities. I am puzzled by the way so many Christian parents can unreflectively leave their children in day care. I witness many families where both parents work, not out of financial necessity, but out of the desire to pursue a higher standard of living without regard for what such preoccupation does to their children. Too often I see teenagers in church whose lives and attitudes are indistinguishable from the secular society in which they live. Repeatedly, I hear of children whose lives are so busy that they have little time for church. It hurts me to hear a father and mother rebuke a child for not performing well in a sport. It pains me to see children being brought into the world by young parents who are still children themselves. It saddens me to see teenagers whose experience tells them that after their "sin" they are no longer welcome in the youth group. But perhaps most devastating is the fact that, in light of this negative environment for children, I often say nothing. Perhaps without fully realizing it, many churches turn a deaf ear to the cries of children and the pleas of the families in which they are being raised. Churches have always been a place where the family has found instruction about the home, but as society puts increasing pressure on the home, those of us in the churches often remain silent.

We must overcome whatever keeps us from hearing the cries of the children in our midst. If we do not address these barriers, we will not be able to respond to the frenzied lives of young children. If we fail to hear those cries, many of those children will not be fully transformed by God. When we hear the cries of the children closest to us, allow them the time to grow spiritually, and give their souls direction, then we make a difference in the world.

Hear God's Heart

I believe the church must advocate even for the children in the families of the local church. In order to hear the cries of all the children in our churches, three obstacles must be removed: inadequate definitions of family, worldly standards that invade the church, and silence about busyness.

Removing Inadequate Definitions of Family

Certain unspoken definitions of family circulate in some church circles. These definitions hold that the only acceptable family is one that has a mother, father, and children. All other family constellations are inferior or incomplete. While such statements are seldom written on the Sunday school chalk board, these are the definitions by which church budgets are set and around which church programs are defined. It is assumed that each family unit will be made up of the three necessary parts (mom, dad, and kids) and other families will need to adjust to those plans.

> ### ‿ ❧
>
> ### *These Children*
> ### *Mean the World*
> ### *to God*
>
> *Jenny and Kim come home every day to an empty house. These fourth and sixth graders get a snack, watch television and play video games, but inside they are afraid. They dread the two hours alone, fearful that somebody will hurt them.*

Many people in church leadership have heard from single parent families, or single people, or grandparents raising grandchildren, or those who speak on behalf of foster children, that there seems to be little planning and room for their kind of family. Those who are unwilling to challenge church leadership often drift away. Such definitions of the family prevent the church from adequately welcoming and ministering to all in their midst. Children in families that do not meet church expectations often cry out, but are seldom heard, even in the church where they attend.

Scripture defines family in a broad way. One family that receives considerable attention in Scripture is the family unit through which God chose to bring his son into the world. The familiar story in Matthew and Luke tells us of the conception by the Holy Spirit. Even Joseph questioned the circumstances, only to be reassured by an angel. All of us have thought about the difficulties Mary had in explaining her pregnancy. Jesus was born without a human father, but was raised by his mother, Mary, and his stepfather, Joseph. The family fled to Egypt when Jesus was young where they were refugees for a period of time. This family would hardly fit into the definition of family unofficially circulating in some churches.

Ephesians 5-6 describes a family with a mother, father, and children. Some might want to use the Ephesians text to argue that the only acceptable family is mom, dad, and the kids, since it treats each of those parties. Such an approach ignores other family constellations that are valued by God. Genesis gives considerable attention to Hagar who becomes a single mother raising her son alone. Moses is raised by foster parents. Samuel is raised by a priest. The wonderful story of the prodigal son is about a man and his two sons. Timothy's parents did not share a common faith. Paul indicates that Timothy's maternal grandmother and mother were the ones that guided him spiritually, not the father as Paul instructs in Ephesians 6:4. James tells us that those who care for orphans live at the core of "pure religion" (1:27). A clear case can be made that God values all kinds of families.

The instructions in Ephesians 5-6 about husbands and wives, or about fathers and children, do not exclude these other kinds of families nor do they make one kind of family normative. God makes provision for those without loving parents (James 1:27) and for those with loving parents (Ephesians 6:1-2). God's people must have the same broad concerns that he has and avoid sending the message that one kind of family constellation is superior to another.

If God conceived of the church as a place big enough for Jews and Gentiles (Ephesians 2:11-22), it was also conceived as large enough to handle all the kinds of families mentioned in the Bible. Orphans, though not mentioned in Ephesians, must be included in the church's view of family. Single parent families, again not cited in Ephesians, appear elsewhere in Scripture and must be included in the church's view of family. A father whose son has become the prodigal, the child whose parents no longer want him, a grandmother and mother trying to raise a Timothy without the active spiritual participation of the father–all these could find a home in the Ephesian church and certainly find direction in the teachings of Ephesians.

Not all families have a father, mother and children. Families as diverse as singles, single again, single parent families, orphaned children, blended families, and children being parented by grandparents need and desire the love and respect of the church community, just as a family made up of a father, mother, and children does. Churches that selectively decide which kinds of families they want to love run counter to the unconditional love taught in the Bible (Romans 8:31-38). In Ephesians, Paul writes to a church community that includes those who are or have been immoral, angry, and drunken. Yet he calls for the church to be a place where all, Jew and Gentile, saint and sinner, can find love. Our churches must imitate that model. Our churches must *be* that model.

Countering the World's Standard

A second obstacle the church must counter is the invasion of the world's standards into the church. The increase in out-of-wedlock births, of divorced homes, of the large number of children of divorce are not just statistics from a pagan world, but often describe the mistakes Christians make. Churches that are winning lost people to Christ find that new Christians have illegitimate children, a series of divorces, problematic marriages, and troubled children.

Ephesians reveals that the early church encountered a similar situation. Ephesians 4:17-5:21 outlines the *moral code* for Christian people. Paul presented the *moral code* because there were those in the Ephesian congregation who were back living as the Gentiles did, just as there are people in our congregations that are living worldly lives. The Ephesian church included those who were indulging in impurity (4:19), anger (4:26), obscenity (5:4), drunkenness (5:18), and other sins listed in Ephesians 4:17-5:21. The fact that after Paul discusses the *moral code*, he turns to the *household code* (Ephesians 5:21-6:9) is instructive. Clearly those who were engaging in the sins that violated the moral code were creating confusion and pain in the family units of the Ephesian church.

How does a church respond when the world's moral standards invade the church? A failure to respond allows this invasion to hinder the church from hearing the cries of the children in these families. If those who sin go unchallenged or are simply ignored and rejected, the church has little opportunity to bring the transforming power of the gospel into the lives of the children involved. Paul offers a twofold response.

First, the church that follows the Ephesian model must teach God's standards. Church must be a place where Christians are taught about sexual purity. The pulpit and classrooms must be characterized by teaching that calls for one man to be married to one woman for life, for no physical or emotional sexual activity outside marriage. The church must be a place where God's hatred of divorce is regularly sounded. The church must be a place where promiscuity is opposed, where adultery and fornication are clearly explained and condemned, where principles of healthy biological families are taught, modeled, and expected.

Second, the church must be a forgiving and healing place. In the midst of the moral code, Paul returns to the issue of forgiveness which he sets at the center of the divine-human relationship in Ephesians 1:7. Then he says, "forgiving each other, just as in Christ God forgave you" (Ephesians 4:32). Broken individuals and dysfunctional families find themselves in need of repair. The church is a place where that can happen. Ephesians 4:17-5:21 is a sobering reminder that Christians often fall short of the standards of God. Paul insists, "that you must no longer live as the Gentiles do" (4:17) indicating he was clearly aware that some of them were living like the Gentiles. In stating this case, the church also becomes a place of healing, a place where we change directions, a place where we move on from past mistakes. The church as a healing place becomes a striking reality. The church is a place of healing for those who have failed.

The church must be a place where those who have failed to reach these standards can change and heal. Although a coach expects each runner to clear every hurdle, that expectation does not keep him from running out to console the one who catches a foot on the bar and sprawls on the track. Children who, through no fault of their own, end up without parents or without one parent can find healing in the church community, where they see intact families, find surrogate models, and replace lost parental figures with significant others.

Offering forgiveness and healing does not mean a retreat from setting high expectations. Keeping the standards high does not require a church to reject all who fail. Offering forgiveness for wrongs does not encourage anyone to do wrong any more than God's sending his son as forgiveness for the world encourages us to do wrong. Christ said both, "Be perfect" *and* "Come to me, all you who are weary and burdened." Christ forgave the woman caught in the act of adultery, but told her to not sin again. Healing and expectations must work in tension in each congregation.

Overcoming the Silence About Busyness

A third obstacle the church must overcome in order to hear the cry of children is its silence about the busy nature of the contemporary family. Church families often live in a frenzy. Spiritual activities can even add to the busyness of life. Many practices regarding children are widely accepted in and out of the church, including homes where both parents work, children in full-time day care, children left unsupervised, children coming home to a house with no parents, influences such as computers and television without parental supervision, and children whose schedules are dictated by demanding teachers and coaches.

My sense is that we in the church are afraid to challenge these activities. We are afraid to ask hard questions: Is this kind of lifestyle good for children? How can we manage the frenzy? To those of us caught up in it, life seems out of control. Who is there to tell the family, "Enough is enough?"

One of the qualities of Jesus' ministry was his ability to withdraw. In Mark 1, Jesus maintains a hectic schedule. The text has one "immediately" after another.[11] Yet in the midst of doing good things, Jesus withdraws (Mark 1:35). On several occasions in the Gospel story, Jesus turns away from the ministry at hand to seek silence, prayer, and solitude. He recognized that life called for a balance between activity and reflection, that he could only do so many things without taking time to be silent.

All around me I see families in a frenzy. Most of the activities they participate in are good. I have no biblical opposition to day care or both parents working. The issue I am raising is that if we follow a Lord who had to occasionally withdraw from good things, why do we believe that our frenzied lifestyle—where we seldom withdraw—is good for us or for our children? What are we teaching our children about life when we permit our busyness to dictate our lives? Where is the voice of the church telling parents to stop? While churches cannot dictate that no church family can have internet access or use day care, the church can be a place where issues are raised:

---

[11]See Mark 1:12, 18, 20, 42 in the Revised Standard Version.

+ Do the reasons both parents work outweigh their obligation as parents?

+ What do children in full time day care need from parents and the church?

+ What are the long-range ramifications of a child too busy with school and extracurricular activities to be involved in the church family?

+ How can children be taught about the dangers of culture and at the same time be prepared to live in the culture?

Cultural practices that directly contradict Scripture or that pose a risk to the parent-child relationship must be challenged in the spiritual community, but that community must also be prepared to guide families in the way to live within that culture as Christians.

After our first child was born, I was driving home from the hospital for some needed sleep, going over the speed limit and weaving in and out of traffic, as was my custom. About halfway home, I realized I was a father. A boy was depending on me. I hit the brakes and stayed in my own lane. I had a responsibility to a child and it changed the way I lived.

Over the years my wife, Sally, and I have put on the brakes in other ways. We protested when cub sports wanted Sunday afternoon. We said no when the boys wanted to be in too many extracurricular activities. We wondered if it was right to have the internet open to them in the playroom. Even as I write this material, I think of the many mistakes we have made. I can't count how many times I have wished I could back up life's tape and relive it. Despite my mistakes, I see where the spiritual community has made up for what I failed to do or could not do. Over the years we have relied a great deal on our congregation for guidance in being parents.

Hear the Call

The church must regain a voice in helping its families raise spiritually-nourished children. Recent studies indicate that forty-five percent of our teenagers do not attend church after they leave our homes. If the church remains mum about issues involving children in our midst, if there is no caring voice calling for and modeling love, no prophetic voice offering a spiritual critique to the demands on the average family, then the loss of our children will continue. At the church where I minister, one out of every five teens comes from a single parent home. If the church ostracizes families that don't fit their preconceived mold and fails to love those who are different, the losses continue to rise. Churches unable to communicate love to families that do not meet their standards of mom, dad, and the kids will be hindered in their ministry to a society that abounds with different kinds of family units. The cultural pressure to be busy and to do everything must be confronted by the spiritual community. Churches unwilling to address the issues that poverty brings to the homes in their communities and unwilling to challenge the unbridled greed and selfishness in affluent families will have little influence on the Christians who pass through their doors.

The Challenge

The God who hears the cry of children being raised in the busyness of the contemporary family has established the church as his ears in today's world. Children mean the world to God. Raising up healthy families is critical to the well-being of children. The ultimate definition of a healthy family comes not from culture or the disciplines promoting physical or emotional well-being, but from Scripture which directs us to spiritual well-being. The church must not be a place where cultural definitions, practices and mandates are accepted uncritically, but a community where God's concerns for the child are taught, discussed, practiced, and applied. When children are raised in a healthy spiritual environment, in both church and home, their lives are changed for the better. Each child raised in that kind of setting has unlimited potential to make the entire world a better place. When we change a child, we change the world.

Exercises

Hear A Child

1. Tell the stories of families you know that have taken steps to protect their children from greed, consumerism, and busyness. Discuss the pros and cons of those steps.

2. Take time to sit down and chart how each family member spends his time in a typical week. Do you see areas where changes need to be made? Pray for wisdom as you consider making these changes.

Hear God's Heart

3. What battles do you observe families fighting today? What does culture say about each issue? What does God say about each issue?

4. Study Ephesians 5-6. What broad principles do you see here that the church must teach to families?

Hear the Call

5. Make a list of critical issues that you want the next family seminar to address. Pray for courage to raise issues that may be unpopular in the current culture.

6. Ask each parent what they need from the church in order to raise spiritually nourished children. Include single parents in the discussion and pay special attention to their needs.

7. The author writes, "healing and expectations must work in tension in each congregation." Discuss how you see this working in your church.

Chapter Six

Why Didn't Anybody Tell Me About Right and Wrong?

Hear A Child

Three of us entered the back door of the variety store on Main Street. It was open lunch period during seventh grade. With a whole hour to eat a sandwich and a bag of chips, we had little else to do, so the three of us made our weekly trip the mile up to Main Street to pick up a few things at the store.

"Pick up" in a literal sense.

I was the guard at one end of the aisle. Fred stood sentry duty at the other end. Jay was the thief because he had the long coat. Nobody was watching. I nodded. Fred nodded. Jay opened his coat and slid in the box of Magic Markers. We regrouped and calmly walked out of the store. One day it was markers, another day baseball trading cards, while other times it was pens or pocket knives. We were thieves. I was a shoplifter.

Shoplifting Ring

None of this went on without intense turmoil inside my head. Every Sunday I sat in Mildred Stutzman's class where we studied Genesis. Trying to sort out right and wrong from Genesis can be confusing for a thirteen-year-old.

"Jacob got the blessing by stealing it. Stealing is wrong, but the blessing is right. God guided the whole process." I was getting blessed by the stealing I was doing, too. My share of the loot was a nice addition to my small allowance.

"Laban cheated Jacob out of his wages. Then Jacob took his property and fled. On the way out the door his wife grabbed Laban's household gods." Our threesome shared one thing in common with Jacob's wife. We never got caught, either.

Despite the dim way in which I understood the Genesis stories, I still sensed something quite wrong with my shoplifting. I knew my parents would highly disapprove, but they didn't know, as I kept my loot strategically placed in my room. Taking something that didn't belong to me seemed wrong even to a kid who came from an unchurched home and knew little about the Bible. But getting something for nothing was a cultural value celebrated by all in our community. Our threesome just created our own way of getting a bargain.

Moral Confusion

Today's children are raised in moral confusion. The movie and music industries promote one standard, the schools another, and the church still another. Children see adults advocate for one way and live a different way. They are given lists of rules, but the rationale for the list is never explained to them. Children pick up on the fact that many rules are self-serving, protecting the interests of those who make them while hurting others in the process.

How do kids learn right from wrong? Who teaches children morality? Who decides what morality is taught? Is it possible to learn right and wrong in the midst of such confusion?

Hear God's Heart

The Bible's first statement about teaching children right from wrong comes in the middle of a culture that failed to teach right from wrong. The first clear statement about morality comes in the midst of tremendous confusion about morality. The beginning of good comes in the middle of a story of a bad place.

The bad place was Sodom. Along with its sister city Gomorrah, it has a long sordid history. By Genesis 13:13 we are told that the "men of Sodom were wicked and were sinning greatly against the Lord." News of the city's wickedness reached heaven. God reports "the outcry against Sodom and Gomorrah is so great and their sin so grievous" that he intends to destroy them (Genesis 18:20-21).

The Bible takes us to the streets of the city where the Sodomites saw Lot welcome two guests for the night. They knocked on Lot's door and asked, "Where are the men who came to you tonight? Bring them out to us so that we can have sex with them" (Genesis 19:5). Sodom had more influence on

Lot than Lot had on Sodom. Instead of repulsing his wicked neighbors, instead of confronting their wicked suggestion, Lot unbelievably offers to give the wicked men his two virgin daughters. The crowd refuses. The angels blind the crowd. Lot and his family flee. The city is destroyed by something with the same effects as a nuclear bomb.

But there was more to the evil of Sodom than the events surrounding Lot. Ezekiel offers a broader perspective.

> As surely as I live, declares the Sovereign LORD, your sister Sodom and her daughters never did what you and your daughters have done. "Now this was the sin of your sister Sodom: She and her daughters were arrogant, overfed and unconcerned; they did not help the poor and needy. They were haughty and did detestable things before me. Therefore I did away with them as you have seen." (Ezekiel 16:48-50).

The sins of Sodom included rape, homosexuality, violence, parental irresponsibility, arrogance, and abuse of the poor. The two cities became the standard of wrong. The rest of Scripture holds them up as the worst of the bad. In Isaiah 1:9 and 3:9, the prophet Isaiah compares sinful Israel to Sodom and Gomorrah. In Jeremiah 49:18, God promises through the prophet Jeremiah that the sinful nation of Edom will become like Sodom and Gomorrah. In Matthew 11:23, Jesus tells the cities who refused to believe in him that they will be worse off than Sodom. In Revelation 11:8, John compares the immorality in Jerusalem to that in Sodom.

From Genesis through Revelation, Sodom and Gomorrah epitomize a society running off track, a people bent on immorality, a culture without morals. How can society maintain a good standard when the legacy of Sodom and Gomorrah is alive and well? What direction do we get for teaching right in the midst of so much wrong?

Two Futures

Just before God destroys Sodom and Gomorrah, there is a significant conversation between Abraham and God. As the two talk on the mountaintop overlooking the wicked cities below, God reveals something incredible to father Abraham.

> When the men got up to leave, they looked down toward Sodom, and Abraham walked along with them to see them on their way. Then the Lord said, "Shall I hide from Abraham what I am about to do? Abraham will surely become a great and powerful nation, and all nations on earth will be blessed through him. **For I have chosen him, so that he will direct his children and his household after him to keep the way of the Lord by doing what is right and just**, so that the Lord will bring about for Abraham what he has promised him." Then the Lord said, "The outcry against Sodom and Gomorrah is so great and their sin so grievous that I will go down and see if what they have done is as bad as the outcry that has reached me. If not, I will know" (Genesis 18:16-21).

Two futures are under discussion, the future of Sodom and the future of Abraham's offspring. The evil of Sodom will lead God to send burning sulphur down on them. In the second future God imagines Abraham's offspring as a mighty, blessed nation. The key to that future comes in verse 19, highlighted in bold, where God reveals that he has chosen Abraham, first proposed in Genesis 12:1-6, to be the one through whom he would bring blessings to the world. Those blessings would flow through Abraham's children.

Abraham is told to "direct" his children. The word *direct* means to appoint or command, to commission or instruct. Jesse *directed* David to take food to his brothers in 1 Samuel 17:20. Boaz used the same word when he *sent* workers to help Ruth (2:9). Moses *directed* parents to obey the law (Deuteronomy 32:46). Here God tells Abraham to *direct* his children "to keep the way of the Lord."

> ####   ❧ ☙
>
> ### *This Child*
> ### *Means the World*
> ### *to God*
>
> *Jonathan is analytical and a quick learner. At age thirteen he has become the family's computer expert. When Mom can't get online, she calls Jonathan. He has no trouble getting onto the internet. In fact, that's where he met "Spandex." "Spandex" is the screen name of a person who claims to be a fourteen-year-old from Florida. They go to a chat room every night. "Spandex" has introduced Jonathan to pornography.*

Then God tells Abraham exactly what to do. As they overlook the wicked cities of Sodom and Gomorrah, God tells Abraham about the high road. He tells him to teach the children about "doing what is right and just."

Doing what was "right and just" was what Sodom and Gomorrah did not do. Doing what was "right and just" was what Lot did not do. Doing what was "right and just" is the first appearance in Scripture of the fundamental principles of morality. The two words appear together nearly a hundred times describing God's moral code. Together they describe the kind of society God seeks to establish in Israel, or in any people of any time.

Justice in Scripture is a courtroom term that calls for fairness, equality, and truth in human relationships. It demands that we go beyond the letter of the law to do what is right and best for another person. *Righteousness* is used in several ways in Scripture. It refers to the way God makes us right and good in his sight. When it is teamed with justice, righteousness describes a kindness and fairness about life. Righteousness when linked with justice means doing the good for another. Justice and righteousness are like a mother and father working together for the benefit of the child, like the army and navy protecting a nation.

The call to do righteousness and justice echoes throughout Scripture. Isaiah told the people "Maintain justice and do what is right" (56:1). Do what is just and right. Jeremiah told the people that God "exercises kindness, justice and righteousness on earth" (9:23-24). God does what is right and just. Later Jeremiah told the king to "do what is just and right" (Jeremiah 22:3). Just in case just and right are misunderstood, Jeremiah makes a list: "Rescue from the hand of his oppressor the one who has been robbed. Do no wrong or violence to the alien, the fatherless, or the widow, and do not shed innocent blood in this place" (22:3). Jeremiah predicts the Messiah will "do what is just and right in the land" (23:5). Another prophet urged, "Give up your violence and oppression and do what is just and right" (Ezekiel 45:9-12).[12]

Jesus put righteousness at the core of his kingdom (Matthew 5:6; 6:33) and critiqued the scribes and Pharisees because their religion had forgotten righteousness and justice (Matthew 23:13-36, especially verses 23 and 28).

Hear the Call

Teaching children what is just and right is often done in the context of an evil society. Abraham and Lot had a long association. After the death of Lot's father, Haran, at an early age (Genesis 11:27-28), Lot came under the influence, first of his grandfather, Terah (Genesis 11:31) and then his uncle, Abraham (Genesis 12:4; 13:1). Even after the two parted company, uncle rescued nephew from certain exile on one occasion (Genesis 14:16). But their separate lives ended quite differently. Abraham advocated with God to save a wicked city for the sake of the righteous people (18:22-33). Lot sought to save his guests from one wickedness by substituting another wickedness (19:5-9).

God told Abraham to instruct children in doing what is right and just in a world that was wrong and unjust. Abraham had to raise children in a world that offered no such instruction, that provided few good examples. We see traces of Sodom and Gomorrah around us every day. The shootings in our schools. The murders in our streets. The car-jackings at our malls. The

[12]Other texts that call for doing what is just and right include 1 Kings 10:9; Isaiah 59:9, 14; Amos 5:24.

child abuse in our homes. The pornography on the internet. The adultery in our marriages. The oppression of our poor. The corruption in our government. From Abraham on, people have been instructing their children about good in a bad world.

Principles versus Lists

Teaching right and wrong involves more than hanging the Ten Commandments on the wall. Teaching about righteousness and justice is more than just making children obey a list of rules. The Bible itself has lists of moral rules, from the Ten Commandments in Exodus 20 to the list of the works of the flesh in Galatians 5:19-21. The lists of rules in the Bible are based on the fundamental principles of Scripture. The Ten Commandments are extensions of the two great commandments (Matthew 22:34-40). The first four of the Ten Commandments explain what it means to love God. The last six of the Ten Commandments explain how we love each other. In teaching the lists, we must not lose sight of what stands behind the lists.

Moses understood this relationship when he explained how children were to be taught about right and wrong.

> These commandments that I give you today are to be upon your hearts. Impress them on your children. Talk about them when you sit at home and when you walk along the road, when you lie down and when you get up (Deuteronomy 6:6-7).

After telling the people to love God with all their heart and soul (Deuteronomy 6:4-5), Moses moved on to the next generation. Just as Abraham was to direct his children, so the Israelites were to teach theirs. Later in the same chapter a case study is supplied:

> In the future, when your son asks you, "What is the meaning of the stipulations, decrees and laws the LORD our God has commanded you?" tell him: "We were slaves of Pharaoh in Egypt, but the LORD brought us out of Egypt with a mighty hand. Before our eyes the LORD sent miraculous signs and wonders–great and terrible–upon Egypt and Pharaoh and his whole household. But he brought us out from there to bring us in and give us the land that he promised on oath to our forefathers. The LORD commanded us to obey all these decrees and to fear the LORD our God, so that we might always prosper and be kept alive, as is the case today. And if we are careful to obey all this law before the LORD our God, as he has commanded us, that will be our righteousness" (Deuteronomy 6:20-25).

A curious question from a child provides an opportunity to rehearse the story of faith and to direct the child to the standards of right and wrong. The word for "righteousness" comes from the same root as the word "right" in God's command to Abraham. The Israelite father was to explain the Ten Commandments and the Mosaic law by telling his children the story of how God had acted in righteousness and justice toward their ancestors. In God's gracious act of mercy to the Hebrew slaves, he did what was right and just. In giving the people the stipulations, decrees, and laws, God was giving substance and direction to their application of the fundamental principles of righteousness and justice.

When we give children lists of rules to obey without any instruction on the principles that prompt the rules, we short-change them. They are not being exposed to the great principles of righteousness and justice. No list of rules can cover all the moral choices a person will need to make in life. The Mosaic law explained the great principles of righteousness and justice to a pre-industrial, agricultural people, but it had its limitations as Paul explains in Romans and Galatians. But righteousness and justice are universal principles that find significance in every decision of life. Jesus often argued with the scribes and Pharisees because they were following a list of rules and he was working out of fundamental principles.

People have always made rules that are extensions of God's principles. Rules such as no card playing, no "R" rated movies, and no shorts often have their origin in something quite fundamental. God told Abraham to direct his children in the fundamental principles. Once those principles are communicated, the rules fall into a broader context and the child is empowered to make good moral decisions even when there is no rule to cover the situation. Morality is not just a list of rights and wrongs, but the ability to think about what is right and wrong in situations we encounter. Our inclination in looking at Sodom and Gomorrah is to make a *list* of what they were doing wrong, while Scripture stresses the *fundamental principles* that their morality ignored.

Lists are made to help us think morally, not to be memorized while the foundations are forgotten. No doubt some of this stands behind Paul's admonition to adults in the Ephesian church: "Fathers, do not exasperate your children; instead, bring them up in the training and instruction of the Lord" (Ephesians 6:4). Our Lord taught about fundamentals. He argued that it all could be reduced to loving God and loving neighbor (Matthew 22:34-40). It meant showing mercy and doing the right things. Any rules taught to children should be in the larger context of the "training and instruction of the Lord."

Walk the Talk

God told Abraham to direct the children to righteousness and justice. Abraham also lived by righteousness and justice. Abraham boldly challenged God to operate by those principles when he asked the LORD to spare the cities if he could find ten righteous people in them. Despite Abraham's shortcomings, God saw that he was a man of faith who tried to live by God's principles.

Children who grow up in the Christian community are exposed to the *teaching* of morality in Bible class and from the pulpit, but they are also taught morality by what the people in the congregation *do*. As a thirteen-year-old with no Bible training, with no long-term church experience, I could see that there was an inconsistency between a church that would not let its teenagers go to any dance and yet never spoke out against adult males reading pornography. I could see that it didn't make sense to respect the law on stealing but not the one on speeding. I could see no logic in telling people not to call God names and then saying nothing about using negative names when it came to a different race.

Even as a teenager I saw the difference between people who broke the moral law because they failed and people who broke the moral law because it was part of a double standard that was permitted. I understood that the older man in the church who used bad language knew that it was wrong and he was working on overcoming it. But I also saw that the man in church who used racist slurs did it because nobody opposed it and he wasn't working on overcoming it at all.

We often accept and teach a moral code that protects our own world view and ignores biblical teaching that we do not personally practice. Children are taught to love, but in the church they see members bitterly attacking a church leader over some point of doctrine. They get two versions of morality, one taught and the other practiced. Children are taught to be sexually pure, but they know of adults who are sexually abusing the children's friends yet leading public prayer on Sunday. These children receive conflicting versions of morality. Children are taught to share and be accepting of other children, but they see adults turn away from helping poor people, or ignoring disabled children, or walking by a person of another race. Children hear the parent complain that nobody from church visited them in the hospital, but know that their parents have never visited anybody else in the hospital themselves. Children are told not to say bad things about other people, yet hear the preacher roasted at lunch every Sunday.

Such dichotomies prevent adults from teaching children right and wrong because they see adults picking and choosing, not a complete willingness to be the kind of people God wants. If we expect our children to be fair and good, we must be a fair and good community.

Modeling Morality

Children who see their parents and people in their church community love the unlovable, forgive the sinner, and encourage the fainthearted grow up to be the same kind of people. Children who see adults sacrifice so they can give, who witness the family putting aside personal pleasures for the sake of others, who are part of a family that tries to live faithfully in an affluent society, who watch the adults accept diversity, become people who follow the same course. Children whose parents live selfishly and greedily become adolescents who want every new toy, go on to become teenagers who expect the church to sponsor ski trips and beach events, and walk into adulthood expecting to be served by the church and community.

Mary and Kimberly learned about morality when they were thirteen. As adolescents they watched the teenagers in the church paint the houses of poor people at work camp, and helped their parents serve underprivileged children at a school store, and looked forward to the day when they could go with the youth group to an impoverished Central American country.

When they were thirteen, I was a sponsor on a mission trip to a government housing project in a city at the other end of the state. Our task was to invite every child in the project to a Vacation Bible School we would conduct. So twenty of us set out to knock on 456 doors. Mary and Kimberly had never knocked on doors. Our leaders assigned us to the same team. I took the first couple of homes, tried to make friends with the families and wrote down the names of the children who were planning to come. After a few houses, Mary was ready. She did a great job and the kids agreed to come. Then Kimberly did the talking. After a few more doors, they were establishing rapport with the kids and their parents quickly and more genuinely than I had. After an hour, they said they would go by themselves. I think I was becoming a liability to them.

As we worked our way from door to door, I kept my eye on the two of them. I saw an inner city woman invite them into her home. I slowed my pace to watch for them to come out. Frankly, I got a bit worried. About forty-five minutes later they emerged. There had been a death in that home. They went in, sat, prayed, listened, held hands, and cried.

At the team devotional that night they retold the story. The experience touched them deeply. They had done a righteous thing. They had represented justice in a world that knew little about fairness. Somehow the experience gave us a bond. Our common experience has created a relationship that has gone beyond a one-week mission trip.

Later I heard that they were in an exclusive club in senior high school. There was an emphasis on dress, appearance, luxury and consumerism. They had good friends in the group, but they felt uncomfortable with the focus. Mary and Kimberly decided to drop out. They wanted to live a different kind of life, practice a morality they had experienced first hand.

The Challenge

Christians often complain about declining moral standards in the culture around them while at the same time ignoring or neglecting to train their own children in matters of justice and righteousness. Many Christians grumble about the behavior of people in their community, yet make little effort to convey to their own children eternal standards of equity and goodness. Right and just living is at the core of our biblical faith and the call to pass these principles on to the next generation is chief among our duties. When children are taught and modeled righteousness and justice, their lives will be changed for the better. They will become a mighty army calling the world to a higher standard.

Exercises

Hear A Child

1. Recall your own childhood training in morality and tell about inconsistencies you saw in the adults around you.

2. As a child, were you given a list of rules or were you taught principles that prompted rules? How did this affect you as a teen?

Hear God's Heart

3. What were the sins of Sodom and Gomorrah? Tell what thoughts you had when you saw the complete list.

4. Do a Bible study on the words "righteousness" and "justice." What did you find?

Hear the Call

5. Since no group of adults is completely consistent in living the morality they teach, discuss what group behaviors allow children to see the difference between the standards and the practice in a positive way.

6. Think about children in your sphere of influence. Would they say your walk and talk are consistent or inconsistent? Why?

Chapter Seven

The Dangers of Exclusiveness

Hear A Child

It was a Sunday-night-after-church potluck meal. The Life Center was crowded with people. Long lines of tables were set up. Home cooked dishes filled the air with a savory aroma. Many visitors had joined us for the occasion. I filled my plate and turned to find a seat. I saw two empty spots.

One vacant chair was beside the news anchor from the television station located next door to our church building. He had brought the television camera over for a brief story on "church fellowships" for the end of their 10:00 P.M. news. With his stylish suit, razor cut hair, and radiant face, it was fairly easy to pick him out. He was known in the community, a lively personality, and fun to be around. I started to move toward him when I spied another open space.

The other empty spot was beside a visiting family. From their dress, I gathered that they were struggling financially. They didn't have on Sunday clothes. The father was dressed in an old University of Tennessee sweatshirt and the mother had on blue jeans that had patches on them. From their behavior, I concluded that they had not been to church much. They were a boisterous bunch whose noise could be heard above the general commotion of the full Life Center. The four little kids had spread food all over the table, the floor, themselves, and their parents. When the father attempted to calm his crowd, I noted that he stuttered. The empty chair beside them was graced with strings of half-eaten spaghetti.

Playing Favorites

It was a split-second decision. With my plate in one hand and my iced tea in the other, I had to find a spot where I was going to eat. I found my seat. I sat next to the news anchor.

Every time I watch the evening news, I see that anchorman. He was at the potluck for a story. He didn't want anything more. I've never seen the family with four kids again. They never returned. They ate at the potluck meal all by themselves. Even the preacher chose not to take the empty seat beside the dirty boy with spaghetti all over his face. Whatever they were seeking at their church visit, they didn't find it.

Later I thought about my response to those four children and their parents. They didn't fit in with our crowd. Their dress was different from mine. Their standards of cleanliness were not the ones we maintain at our house. Differences in discipline, background, occupation, language, and lifestyle were all apparent.

My brief encounter with them made me think back to my own childhood. I wondered how different this family with four kids was from our family with six kids. It made me wonder if some preacher in my own childhood hadn't reacted to our family like I did to this one.

For Members Only

As I pondered my decision not to sit with this family, I wondered how those four kids felt about their visit. Did anybody make them feel welcome in our congregation? Did they feel any warmth or acceptance from us? Did they receive a blessing from coming? Would their singular childhood memory of being in church be different from my memories of attending Vacation Bible School each summer but never being invited to church? Did they plead with their parents the following week, "Let's go back to that church with the spaghetti?"

Behind all those questions are deeper ones. Why do we sometimes act like the church is an exclusive club? Why do we stay away from people who are different from us? Why are we afraid to let our children be around children that are different from them? What do our own children learn from this sense of exclusivism?

Clubs keep out the unwanted and accept only the favored. Clubs come in a variety of forms. Sports teams accept only those with athletic ability. Many of us remember not "making the team." Schools accept students based on intelligence. Some of us got the letters from a college that basically said, "Not you, not here." Country club memberships favor certain income levels or career standards. Nearly everybody has been turned away from some establishment because they could not produce the membership card.

Hear God's Heart

The church is not a club. Its founder never intended for it to cater to only the favored. Those who support *excluding* people from God's family face a God who wants to *include* folks in his family. That's what happened to Jonah in the Old Testament. God wanted a group of people included. Jonah did his best to exclude them. Finally, God and the prophet came face to face over the issue of who decides whom God chooses.

As the book opens, God tells the prophet to travel east to preach to the wicked city of Nineveh. Jonah promptly heads west. Through a storm, a crew of sailors, and a fish, God redirects his prophet toward Nineveh where Jonah obediently delivers his eight word sermon. In chapter 3, everybody in the city repents and turns to God who offers them forgiveness. Jonah's response at the beginning of chapter 4 is amazing:

But Jonah was greatly displeased and became angry. He prayed to the LORD, "O LORD, is this not what I said when I was still at home? This is why I was so quick to flee to Tarshish. I knew that you are a gracious and compassionate God, slow to anger and abounding in love, a God who relents from sending calamity. Now, O LORD, take my life, for it is better for me to die than to live." But the LORD replied, "Have you any right to be angry?" (Jonah 4:1-4).

When Jonah hears that God accepts the repentance of the wicked people in Nineveh, he explodes in anger, telling God that the possibility that they would repent and become God's people was exactly the reason he didn't want to go in the first place. Jonah wants to die. If God is going to save people that Jonah thinks should not be accepted, then he has no reason to live. Jonah wants to be judge of whom God can save or not save. Seeing that God won't let him dictate policy, he chooses to die. But the God who is "slow to anger" will be gentle even with the prophet who was so quick to anger. God questions Jonah's right to call the shots.

After this exchange between God and the prophet, God sends a vine to shade Jonah but removes it the next morning. God decides who is included in his salvation just as he decides who gets the shade of the vine. The loss of the vine upsets Jonah again. The prophet can't see that the salvation of the city is far more important than the vine or even the prophet's personal comfort. If God is going to save people he doesn't like and take away a vine he does like, then Jonah doesn't want to live. Jonah wants to be the gatekeeper on whom God lets in. If grace is not dispensed according to Jonah's agenda, then he would like to leave. The book ends with God's final statement telling us that no one, not even a prophet of God, has a right to decide whom God lets in.

The people in Nineveh were wicked. That issue is not at debate. What is up for discussion is, who decides whom God favors? Jonah wants the job. He wants to exclude those God has decided to include. As membership director he wants God's club limited to those he approves. The inclusive God of the book of Jonah opposes all those who are exclusive. God includes even the formerly wicked Ninevites and the rebellious prophet. He is an inclusive God.

God Includes All

From the beginning God called his people to be open to all. Note what I have bolded in God's promise to Abraham "I will bless those who bless you, and whoever curses you I will curse; and **all peoples on earth** will be blessed through you" (Genesis 12:3). The blessing was passed through an exclusive group, the descendants of Abraham, but the blessing was extended to all people. God's plan was to draw all people to himself by showing them, through Abraham's clan, what it was like to be blessed by God.

When Abraham's descendants became a nation, he called them a "kingdom of priests," who would serve as God's voice to the world, because "all the earth is mine" (Exodus 19:5-6). The world was God's congregation, the Israelites were his representatives. They did not have an exclusive claim on God, only the calling to be God's conduit of grace to all.

Jesus echoed the call to Abraham when he told his apostles "Therefore go and make disciples of all nations" (Matthew 28:19). A few days later in Acts 2 that mission became reality when people from fifteen different countries were issued an invitation. From there the mission to all the world picked up steam. Nobody was to be excluded.

We have no biblical right to make the church an exclusive club. The Corinthian church had trouble with this basic tenet of Christianity. Paul explained:

But God chose the foolish things of the world to shame the wise; God chose the weak things of the world to shame the strong. He chose the lowly things of this world and the despised things–and the things that are not–to nullify the things that are, so that no one may boast before him (1 Corinthians 1:27-29).

Behind these words to the Corinthians is an inclusive God who often chooses those the world would exclude. Peter struggled with the issue of letting in the Gentiles in Acts 10, but God made it clear that the door was open. The dream about the clean and unclean animals in a heaven-sent sheet allowed Peter to see that his exclusivism was wrong. James critiqued the churches that welcomed the rich and shunned the poor (James 2:1-7). Giving the best pew to the best dressed ran against all that God stood for. There are no reserved seats at church. Nobody has dibs on any pew. Every person is to have opportunity to sit in every seat.

God's openness to all people is at the core of Scripture. Jesus promised that on the cross he would draw "all men" to himself. All are welcome. Nobody is turned away. No child, no matter how dirty or different or difficult or distracting, falls outside the clear biblical mandate to be open to all.

Guarding Against the World's Influence

After stating God's interest in all people, another strong biblical point must be stressed. God's mission to be open to all people contains the regular warning not to let the world influence us more than God influences us. Moses told the Israelites not to marry the pagan women of Moab (Numbers 25) just as Ezra warned a later group not to tie the knot with the Canaanites

(Ezra 9). The concern in both cases was not to exclude these people from God's blessing, but to keep their pagan views from turning the people away from God.

Paul urged the Corinthians not to be mismatched with unbelievers (2 Corinthians 6:14). Christians have argued about the implications of what he intended, but the purpose was clear. Too much unrestricted exposure to ungodliness can pull us away from our faith.

James gets to the heart of the matter: friendship with the world is too large a cost to pay (James 4:4). We must be in the world, but not of it. We must be open to the world, but not ruled by it. We must invite those in the world to come to God, but must not allow their ungodliness to be baptized with them. Lot permitted his family to be more influenced by Sodom than they were by God (Genesis 18-19).

These two biblical doctrines put us in tension. How can we be open to the world but not influenced by it? How do children fit into this cautious openness? What does it say about children already in the church? Our children are not perfect, but how do we protect them from being influenced by ungodliness? What does it say about children outside the church who often feel unwelcome in some congregations?

Hear the Call

A great unspoken fear paralyzes churches. We fear that if we bring in children who are different from our children that our children will suffer. Dirty kids will make our kids dirty. Children from dysfunctional homes may have a disease they will transmit to our kids. Our children might hear swear words. We might be willing to associate with the outcast ourselves, but the protective hedge we put around our own children prevents us from risking their association with the child who is different.

If we are a white church, we fear too many black children will chase away the white families. If we are a black church, we fear that too many whites will take away our identity. We are afraid that too many new kids will radically change the nature of our congregation. Children infected with the HIV virus could end up in our nursery. If too many unschooled children come into our Sunday school, we will lose all sense of discipline.

These fears raise questions. Are we more influenced by the world's sense of exclusivism than we are

 Cʒ ꙮ

These Children Mean the World to God

After school a senior high student approached two junior high boys, Nathaniel and Chris. For several weeks they had been attracted to this older student who showed them attention. Now he urged them to try some drugs. The two boys were caught off-guard, but said "no." The reason they declined was because of Jeremy. A 21-year-old ex-con, Jeremy taught the seventh graders each Sunday. All his students knew his story. One night at a local fast food restaurant he had bought some drugs. His drug use had gotten him into trouble with the police. He had served two years. His students got the message.

by God's insistence on inclusivism? Do we want to be a club like
the ones we see all around us or do we want to be like the New
Testament church? When it comes to children outside our
churches, how can we be a part of letting God have more influence on them than the world now does?

Overcoming Our Fears

Welcoming outsiders and maintaining our faith are not mutually exclusive. But welcoming outsiders and maintaining our
faith may cause us to be more reflective of what Scripture calls
us to be. God calls us to take up our cross and follow him. Cross-
bearing is risky and dangerous. The only thing more dangerous
than bearing a cross is refusing to bear one at all. Ministry is
often dangerous. Many believe that the majority of the apostles
met violent deaths. Jesus ended up on a cross. The church has
been persecuted from the beginning. Safety has never been a
major goal of the Christian faith.

That is not to say that ministry should be done carelessly. We
do not arrogantly walk into the jaws of death. We do not easily
toss any life aside. Churches have found ways to minister to children who are HIV-positive without risk. Many churches have
nursery policies that offer protection to all children. Leaders
who have the spiritual development of the church at heart will
place adults in each classroom who have been trained to deal
with children who come from a variety of backgrounds. A fundamental principle of the gospel is that everybody can change.
A child who has been schooled in the ways of the world can be
re-schooled in the ways of God. It may not be easy. It may take
effort. It may involve risk. But it can be done.

The Dangers of Isolation

The fear of exposing our children to the world is balanced by the danger of raising children in isolation from the world. Children must be prepared to face all of life. Children willingly or unwillingly will eventually confront the dangers of the world. Children raised in isolation become teenagers unable to cope with the real world. Too many unprepared prodigals die in the foreign country. Too many children succumb to their first encounter with sin. Too many children leave our churches naive about the real world.

Our children will encounter the world of wickedness and danger. What better place to prepare our children for that encounter than in our homes and our churches? When children are exposed to all elements of life in a situation where responsible adults can help them understand and interpret such events, they grow up better prepared to deal with life.

A friend had two sons and two daughters. They worked in urban ministry. Their house was like a motel. Pregnant teens, ex-convicts, drunken young men, and addicted women were regulars around their table and with their young children. When I asked Bill why they exposed their children to people with these kinds of issues, he told me that they had two reasons. One, they wanted their children to see the worst the world had to offer while they were in the protective environment of their own home. That way they would grow up without fears of the unknown and without the ill-preparedness of being raised in isolation. Two, he wanted his children to see first hand the terrible consequences of wicked living. He wanted his daughters to see the trauma of a pregnant teenager and the terrible feelings after a drunken orgy and the agony of coming off of a drug high. He felt there was no better or safer way to prepare them for life. So their home was a welcome center for the rejected and the outsider.

The Dangers of Exclusivism

Exclusivity is not only unbiblical, it is also dangerous. It is dangerous in two ways: for what it teaches our own children, and for how it fails the unchurched children growing up around us.

Dangers to Our Own Children. Children raised in churches that operate like country clubs grow up to respond in one of two disastrous ways. First, as adults they become more exclusive than their parents. Children who have never been taught about God's mission to all people become Jonahs. Children who are instructed that they are privileged and that certain people should never have access to what they have, become like the people James critiques. They become so self-focused that the "take up my cross and follow me" call has no real meaning. They keep all of God's blessing for themselves. They narrow the scope of the gospel to people they approve. They become more exclusive than their parents.

The second disaster is that the children see past the exclusiveness of their upbringing and decide to reject the faith because of what they perceive to be its narrowness. In my work, I encounter large numbers of people who left our fellowship when they became adults. The reason is almost always because they were taught a human-devised narrowness that totally contradicts the open arms of God. It is striking that nearly half of the children raised in the church leave it when they reach adulthood. Prejudice, racism, bigotry, favoritism, and intolerance are terrible lessons to teach a child, lessons that lead the child to future difficulties.

Dangers to the Children Around Us. There are unchurched children all around us whose lives are up for grabs. They could grow up to be the next Moses or Paul or David, or they might as adults become the next Hitler or Mussolini or Stalin. In twenty years they might be the governor of our state or the preacher of your church. They might become the person who robs our house or the convict who murders your friend. Right now those children have an undecided future. They are open. They are impressionable.

But one thing is absolutely sure. The children who have no status or voice or privilege will grow up. If they are excluded as children from places where godliness is valued and righteousness is taught, there is little chance that they will become people of God. They will learn either from a Sunday school teacher or from a gang leader. They will be influenced by a deacon or a drug dealer. They will learn to respect the Lord or curse him. But they will grow up.

Little girls in our community could be the next Sarah or Hannah or Mary. One might be a future President or a next generation Sunday school teacher. They could also become the next act on the stage at the exotic dance club or a drug user. One thing is absolutely sure: the dirty, outcast children will grow up.

Rejected by the Church

A good friend of mine, Timmy, grew up in the 1950s in a Memphis housing project. His father left the home when Timmy was a child, so life was hard. At age thirteen, Timmy decided to go to church. It was summer and he had no shoes. Alarmed church members watched him enter, convened a hasty committee in the foyer, and sent a representative to ask him to leave. No shoes, no service.

Deserted by his father, he now felt rejected by the heavenly Father. The banishment would dominate his thinking for twenty-five years. When we met, he was agnostic. After several years of study and prayer, he finally gave his life to Christ. Now he teaches children in the struggling public school system. Because he was turned away from a church, twenty-five years of his life were lost for the cause of good. Timmy sits in front of me every Sunday in Bible class. Every time I see him I am reminded not to turn away any child.

Timmy's story reminds me of my own. It reminded me of the way I felt around Susan Wexler. I felt inferior to Susan. In fact, I believed I was inferior. Her father owned the town's best jewelry store on Main Street. We never went there because it was too expensive. Ironically, the Wexlers lived almost across the street from us. That was as close as we came. They had a beautiful stone home with a winding driveway and ample back yard. Our house was always under construction, had two different colors of shingles on the roof and for a while had a twenty-foot I-beam extending out the front like a boy sticking out his tongue at passers-by.

I always wondered what Susan thought of that I-beam. More than that, I wondered what Susan thought of me. I felt inferior to Susan and the whole privileged class of people of which she was a part. She was a grade above me in school, but miles ahead in the view of society. She was in. I was out. She was well-dressed. I dressed like a working boy. She had a stone house. Ours stuck out like a sore thumb. She circulated among the rich and influential. I don't think I circulated much at all.

I understand why her crowd would never accept me. We were not equals. She lived a life of privilege. I did not. I was on the outside and I understood why I was outside. What I didn't understand was Mildred Stutzman. She, too, was part of the privileged class. They owned land, had nice houses, and fine cars. I never expected to be invited to the Wexler's for lunch, but was surprised beyond description when Mildred invited me to their house for lunch. Mildred understood the God who included all, the God who championed the orphans, the God who treated all people fairly. Because Mildred understood God, I was invited to lunch. And because I was invited to lunch, I learned about the bread of life.

The Challenge

God's vision includes every person. Our natural inclination is to protect our own by erecting fences. But the process of keeping others out weakens the structure of who we are, prevents us from raising our own children to be like God, and denies us the opportunity of teaching those outside our walls. When we insist that God's ministry knows no boundary, we transform the lives of our own children and create ways for God to change isolated and hurting children everywhere. Children who grow up like I did are often excluded. When they are included, they change and through them God transforms the whole society.

Accepting a Few Unwanted Children

In the early eighties, a Sunday school class in Memphis wondered how they could serve the unserved and unwelcome. They began what they called Parents' Night Out. They invited parents of disabled children to bring their children to the church building for four hours on Friday night where babysitting would be provided free. Parents of such children often have a difficult time finding suitable sitters or have financial restrictions that prevent them from taking a break from the intensive demands of caring for their offspring.

This ministry solves both of those problems. The church has always had enough people trained in special education to provide guidance to the caring people who serve the children. The program is free. Every Monday the church phone rings with parents eager to have their children involved in this program. For twenty years the ministry has served disadvantaged children.

The program costs the church almost nothing. The budget includes a small amount for postage to invite these families to special events. It has benefitted the congregation immensely. Many of our members make it a family affair. They find that their healthy children grow in compassion, sensitivity and gratitude by being care-givers to these disabled children. It proves to be a simple, but effective, way to hear the cry of children.

Not all children are created equal in the eyes of society. There will always be the people of privilege who look down on the underclass. There will be children like the spaghetti-covered visitors at our church potluck that nobody wants to embrace. But throughout Scripture these are the very children God embraces.

From Ishmael to the outcasts that made up the Corinthian church, God accepts the outsider. One question remains: Do we act more like our society that excludes and refuses, or do we imitate our father who welcomes and accepts?

Exercises

Hear A Child

1. Share whether you felt welcomed or rejected as a child. List the issues that such status created in your life.

2. Share examples you've witnessed of children being accepted or rejected at your congregation.

Hear God's Heart

3. Jonah in the Old Testament and Peter in the New Testament both struggled with exclusivism. God helped both become inclusive in dramatic ways. What were the ultimate results of Jonah's and Peter's changed hearts? What implication does this have for you? For your church?

Hear the Call

4. Make a list of children in your area that regularly experience rejection. Ask those in the congregation who work with children to expand the list. What ministry possibilities are suggested?

5. What specifically makes a family or a church exclusive? Inclusive?

6. Arrange a forum to discuss the fears we have about our children being around children we consider unacceptable. Who might be asked to speak? What topics should be discussed? What biblical doctrines must be presented?

Chapter Eight
The Alone

Hear A Child

We met at Café Olé in the Memphis Cooper-Young neighborhood to discuss the ministries of the congregation where I preach. My friend directs a local agency that helps families adopt and foster unwanted children. Over a taco he put the question to me directly. "What is your congregation's role in helping parentless children?"

I told him that such children were not even in our field of vision. We had certain goals as a church, but focusing on abandoned children was not one of them. We cared for our own kids, sent missionaries to children around the world, had a yearly Vacation Bible School, but aside from a couple of line items in the budget, we did little more than offer a small stipend to child care agencies.

Such children were not even in our field of vision. Perhaps it would be more accurate to say that parentless children were not in *my* field of vision. I'd always seen children as an unavoidable issue in ministry, but not the focus of God's work. Beyond that I had pushed *orphaned* kids even further off the map. Two things forced me to change my mind.

A Conversion of the Heart

Randy Becton was always paying attention to the Ukrainian children. We were partners in several short-term mission trips. When we had a program, Randy would move toward the children, bend his 6'8" frame over and win their affection. I admired his ability to connect with kids, but thought that he was wasting valuable campaign time. We should focus on adults.

Then somebody told me that Ukrainian culture placed a great emphasis on children, that those who wanted to win the hearts of the adults should focus on the kids. So when I got up to speak in the medical college lecture hall in December 1992, I began my lesson by asking all the children in the vast auditorium to come to the front to have their picture taken with me. About fifty-five children came up. I picked up a little three-year-old boy named Alosha, and held him. Then I looked over and saw that Randy had joined the photo. My first response was, he's stealing my show. Then something snapped–not the camera, but something inside of me. I realized that I viewed children the wrong way. Putting children into convenient slots in my theology would not do. Randy never said a word to me, but he communicated a tremendous message. By the way he treated his own children and by how he was drawn to the fifty-five Ukrainian children, I began to see the link between what Randy and Camilla did at home, what he did in Ukraine, and how it all connected to Scripture.

A Conversion of the Mind

The second thing that changed my mind occurred a couple of years later in my own office. Tom Burton and Nick Boone, representing Christian Child and Family Services Association, a consortium of about sixty Christian child care agencies, drove to Memphis from Nashville with a question. Would I be their national spokesperson?

I felt like a hypocrite. Why me? If they knew what I had thought about Randy Becton stealing the show in the photo op, if they knew how I had done ministry in Milwaukee, if they had heard me tell my friend at Café Olé that "orphaned children are not even in our field of vision," if they knew any of that, they would have gone home.

I Will Not Forget

Then I realized what God was doing. I had been wrong. As a leader in the church I had been wrong to ignore children, and especially wrong to ignore the parentless. Under my leadership little had been done to help the disenfranchised. I recalled a line from a speech that Ira North had given in the 1960s: "The benevolence work of the average church can be done by one person on a Sunday afternoon in fifteen minutes." He wasn't far off the mark with the churches I had known. After talking with Tom and Nick, I learned that most child care agencies turn away four of every five children who come to them because they lack the money or the foster parents to help. I began to wonder. What is

the church's responsibility to orphans? Is it a ministry extrane-
ous to the real work of the church? What is the biblical teaching
about orphans?

Hear God's Heart

The word the Old Testament uses to describe children without parents comes from a root that means "lonely" or "unique."
The word often appears with widow suggesting the vulnerability that the parentless child and husbandless woman share in
common. They are children without a father (Lamentations 5:3)
who have no helpers in life (Job 29:12). Many times this word
refers to war orphans. Micah accused the wicked rich in
Jerusalem of taking away the blessing, or land, of the children
(Micah 2:9). Most likely these children were the orphans of the
120,000 Judean men who died in the invasion led by Pekah (2
Chronicles 28:5), or the many who fell in the subsequent mili-
tary activity of the Edomite and Philistine armies (2 Chronicles
28:17). Lamentations 5:3 also refers to war orphans. Probably
many of these children had war widow mothers. Unscrupulous
people were taking advantage of these vulnerable children.

The Greek word for parentless children is the word from
which we derive the English word "orphan." It means to be
deprived of one's parents.

The English word "orphan" came to mean a child that had
lost both parents. Even that word has fallen into disuse as we
use a new vocabulary of "children in foster care" or "child welfare" or "unloved children" to describe a new kind of unparented child. Like the Old Testament children who had a living

mother, many of these children today have living mothers and fathers, but they are parents who have quit being parents, who through neglect, abuse, and abandonment have left their offspring vulnerable. They are parents who are casualties of spiritual warfare.

The Great Adoptive Father

Psalm 68:5 captures the Bible's core value with regard to unparented children: "A father to the fatherless, a defender of widows, is God in his holy dwelling." Human children who lose their earthly parents find a replacement in God. As God sees children without parents, he becomes their adoptive parent and watches over them from heaven.

Orphans are under the special care of God. According to Isaiah 49:14-15, a mother may not love a child at her breast, but God loves all of us despite what our mothers do. Even if a mother aborts the child in her womb, God will not abort any of us. The love that God gives to all of us, he gives in a special way to orphans. God will not desert those of us who have a father and mother, but God pays special attention to children without either.

According to the Old Testament, God does six things for orphans: (1) God is the *father* to those who have no father (Psalm 68:5); (2) God *helps* those who have no parents (Psalm 10:14); (3) God *defends* the orphans (Deuteronomy 10:18; Psalm 10:18; Proverbs 23:10-11); (4) God *sustains* the fatherless (Psalm 146:9); (5) God promises to *protect* even the orphans of Israel's enemies (Jeremiah 49:11); (6) His heart is filled with *compassion* for the parentless child (Hosea 14:3).

Because of God's self-appointed role as guardian to parentless children, he calls on the spiritual community to assist him. As I write this chapter, there are ten thousand such children in my home state, one unwanted child for every 539 adults, enough children to fill a small town. These are not children who have been adopted, or placed in loving homes, but children whose parents are the State. There are one-half million such foster children in the entire nation. The numbers will change with location and the passing of time, but the problem of mothers who have forgotten and fathers who have forsaken their children remains. Nearly half of the births in the city where I live are to women without husbands. When unwed mothers-to-be are making decisions about whether to parent their unborn child, abort the baby, or place the newborn in an adoptive home, the spiritual community must be there to speak and act on behalf of the unborn children.

The God who promised not to forsake or forget any one of us has a plan. The plan for caring for neglected children is spelled out in the Bible. Almost all of the verses are from the Old Testament. The cultural specifics of providing for these neglected children may change, but the principles found in the Old Testament remain vital for our time.

God-Appointed Defenders

When children lost a parent, the Old Testament makes it clear that the responsibility of caring for the child was passed on to the spiritual community. God told Israel to do five things for orphans. The first two responsibilities offered basic support. (1) In that agrarian society orphans were to be allowed to *glean* in the field (Deuteronomy 24:19-21). (2) Beyond that basic sustenance, each village provided additional *support*. According to Deuteronomy 14:28-29; 26:12, the people were to give every third year's tithe to the poor. For example, in the first year the people would give ten percent, which went to the temple in Jerusalem; in the second year they would repeat that process; in the third year they gave their tithe to the village officials who provided for the poor, including the orphans. One third of the Israelite budget went to the poor. (3) Besides these two regulations for basic support, the law also provided a guaranteed *seat* at the feast days. The festival days in Jerusalem were crowded with people. It would be easy for the vulnerable to be denied a place. But the law demanded that the Israelites save seats for orphans. It was God saying, they will be in church, they will be cared for by the spir-

---

ଔ ଠ

This Child Means the World to God

Tasha lives with a caring Christian family. This eighteen-month old has a congenital heart condition discovered after her father walked out on the family and her mother left her on a neighbor's porch. Her foster parents have taken her case to court six times in the last year to ask the judge to order the state to pay for a process that will correct the defect. For the sixth straight time the judge has refused to hear the case. This little girl may die in the middle of a city that offers some of the world's best pediatric care.

itual community (Deuteronomy 16:11-14). (4) Although there is no Mosaic law about *adoption*, there clearly was that practice. Job took orphan children into his own home (Job 31:16-18). (5) The prophets and psalmist called for *fairness in the courts* for parentless children (Isaiah 1:17; Psalm 82:3). The only New Testament verse about orphans calls for Christians to *look after* widows and orphans (James 1:27) in keeping with the principles outlined in the Old Testament.

There is no one Bible text to which we turn for information on orphans. But the treatment of orphans is mentioned in numerous places throughout Scripture and, when we gather all these together, there is a comprehensive picture. When children end up without parents, the spiritual community takes over. It's not right in God's eyes for children to be without some kind of parents. No child should have to go without a mommy and daddy. Even if parents are gone, the community must see to that child.

Hear the Call

The specifics of the Old Testament texts on the fatherless have passed away. We are not required to tithe, leave gleanings, or save seats at the Passover feast. But the God behind those laws is still a God of justice and righteousness, who calls his people to look after the orphans and widows. The principle of the spiritual community caring for the disenfranchised spans the testaments. The Gospel of Luke has considerable focus on the downcast. The early church cared for the poor. Paul engaged in fund raising for the poverty-stricken. James critiqued some for their lack of concern for the lowly. Today's church must continue to show mercy to the vulnerable, especially those who have been forgotten and forsaken by their parents.

The Indictment

The most vulnerable children in our world are the ones who have no one, no support network, no family, no mother, no father to care for them. They are the epitome of weakness and vulnerability. As Christian people, there is no way we can claim our Christian identity and leave the weakest of all without help. To claim to worship God and then neglect the children he has adopted is hypocrisy.

Children without parents are often not in a church's "field of vision." Complaints about the parking lot and concerns about the temperature in the auditorium often take precedence over what concerns the heart of God. Churches that fail to care for orphans are not practicing pure religion. They are ignoring a God-ordained mandate. Helping orphans is not an optional part of the budget. It should be at the core of what the church is about.

I have come to believe that we are under indictment for the way we allow our culture to ignore unwanted children. God has made it clear that this matter is close to his heart, but it is far from the hearts of some Christians and many churches. We often convey the sense that unwanted children are not our concern, or that the few dollars we send their way are sufficient, or that we can go on living affluent lifestyles without concern for the parentless children who live in every single city in America. I seldom hear a prayer in any church service for unwanted children.

Few tears are shed for the children in today's foster care system who are being denied their rights in our court system.

Children who have been deserted by their parents or forcibly removed from their abusive homes by the state have little voice in the entire process. Who speaks for them? Why are the churches silent about these unfortunate children? What can we do? How can we help? Let me point in two directions.

Ownership

First, churches must take ownership of this problem. Serving God by caring for his special children is not limited to line items in the church budget for children's homes. Christians must claim ownership of this matter. We must find some way to be involved as God's people in serving as surrogate parents for the world's unloved children.

Discussions about orphans often raise tension levels because there is a subtle implication that all of us should become adoptive parents or take in foster kids. Job opened his home in that way, but there were many great people of faith in the Bible who never took in a fatherless child. We are not told that bringing such children into our homes is part of every Christian's life. No one should feel guilty for making a decision against such a course.

Yet God does call certain families to this kind of ministry. Making a difference in the life of one child may be what God prepares some people to do. Many child care organizations offer classes and one-on-one sessions that allow Christians to explore this option before making a decision.

Although we may not share our extra bedroom with a parentless child, we do share in God's responsibility to children. Unwanted children need school teachers, nurses, doctors,

Sunday school teachers, camp counselors, mentors, and social workers who care for them in a special way. Those who are foster parents and adoptive parents must have a larger community around them that enables them to take in a child. Many churches and almost all communities of any size have ways for each one of us to be involved in sustaining, caring, and providing for children who have no parents.

Such concern can be quite simple. Our elders, staff, and spouses gathered one evening for fellowship and prayer. As we put together our prayer list, one of the elders' wives brought up Don and Denise who were fostering a child in their home. She announced that the child's father had gone to court to get the child back. There was an audible "Oh, no" that went through the group of forty-five people. They knew the situation. They remembered that this father had dropped the baby on the street and did not return. They knew it was a power play, but not to be taken lightly. The "Oh, no" and the fervent prayers that followed reflected how that one little, unwanted baby had taken over a room in the hearts of these church leaders. As soon as the announcement was made, they fell immediately into prayer.

After that prayer I thought of my conversation at Café Olé about orphans not being in "our field of vision." I was wrong. Wrong in more ways than one. The leaders with whom I served had one foster child right in the center of their "field of vision."

Support Those at the Front

Besides accepting our responsibility for unwanted children, the second task we can undertake is to support those on the front lines. Christian organizations exist across the nation to care for unwanted children. Christians have always been at the forefront of efforts to help unwanted kids. Child care agencies and urban ministries have had a special focus on such children.

Renee Vail is one such child. She grew up in Northeast Arkansas. Not long ago Renee painted a self portrait. A mother holds a child, her right hand cradling the child's head as it rests on her breast. But the colors are dark and the faces troubled. Something is not right. The contrast between the figures and the tone of the painting alerts us to a problem. Renee explained the painting in a poem called "Childhood Dreams." The first stanza tells of her early life:

> The dreams were big and beautiful, but died of thirst.
> The ambitions great but withered in the sun
> The ideas refreshing but blew away like dust
> They lay there lifeless dead from neglect.

Renee was an orphan. Her dreams were crushed by her exposure and vulnerability. How could a child without a mother and father accomplish what she most wanted? The second stanza completes the story:

> Suddenly raindrops fell from heaven replenishing the soul.
> The rain fell and the wind whispered, you can, you will, I will show the way.
> So it was and the childhood dreams blossomed once more.

Renee tells in poetic form of encountering caring Christians who became her parents, who restored her dreams, and who led her to adulthood. Now a parent herself, Renee is accomplishing her dreams.

People Making a Difference

It looked like she had been forsaken or forgotten. Then raindrops fell from heaven. She found a heavenly father in more than one way. Renee found something special in people who care for unwanted children. So have I.

The first time I attended the Christian Child and Family Services Association conference, it was in San Francisco with the theme of *Building Bridges*. As I visited with and listened to these people who care for children around the nation, several things occurred to me.

First, they are knowledgeable people. They not only know children, but they are well-versed in the laws about children and in the psychology and sociology of caring for hurting kids. They are not only ministers, but administrators; not only servants of Christ, but students of the best literature on dealing with children.

Second, they know what it is like to be uncared for. I was struck by how many involved in child care were cast aside by their own parents. Not all of them, by any means, but many of those who lead in child care know first-hand what they are doing. I was struck by how many said something like, "I grew up at Boles Home," or "Agape placed me in a Christian home when I was thirteen."

Third, they are dedicated people. Most of them serve as CEOs of large agencies that care for hundreds of children, yet nearly every one of them has adopted a child or has served as a foster parent. Their lives match their words.

Fred and Marva Dycus are a case in point. They have several children of their own, but are in the process of adopting three siblings from Ethiopia whose parents died two years ago. They spoke with some urgency since the oldest of the three will soon be too old to be adopted according to Ethiopian law.

The most impressive aspect of San Francisco was not the Golden Gate Bridge, or Fisherman's Wharf, but the hearts and work of Christians who care for children.

Not everyone can be Fred and Marva Dycus who create a place in their home for an unloved child, but all can create a place in their hearts for deserted kids. When Christians hear the biblical truth about orphans from the pulpit and lectern, see that unparented children are welcomed in the spiritual community, and witness the encouragement given to families involved in foster care or adoption, then God makes a room in their heart for parentless children just like he did in mine.

The Challenge

The way in which any community–whether a church or a city–cares for its most vulnerable members reveals the character of that community. Changing the life of an orphaned child may seem insignificant in light of a global context, but it is not. Such care represents core values. When a church believes orphans are important and that caring for them is central to their vision, not only are the lives of the unloved children changed, but such a perspective reflects a much larger transformation taking place for good in a degenerate world.

God made orphans his responsibility. Will we seek to be like him by taking on the same role?

Exercises

Hear A Child

1. Tell about a child you know that lost his or her parents in some way.

2. Tell about a time you felt parentless.

Hear God's Heart

3. How are God's laws about orphans being violated by Christians today?

4. What does James 1:27 mean to your life?

Hear the Call

5. In what ways does your church show mercy to orphans?

6. Take time to pray for the foster parents and their children that you know. Write them a note of appreciation and encouragement.

Chapter Nine
A Place for All Children

Hear A Child

When I was fifteen, I worked on Stutzman's potato farm. Mildred Stutzman led me to God when I was thirteen. Guy Stutzman introduced me to the work place when I was fifteen. Along with several other teenagers from church, my job was to load sacks of potatoes onto a truck. Between trucks we didn't have much to do. While we waited we often got into mischief.

One day another boy from church named Whitey and I were wrestling. Mr. Stutzman had told us repeatedly not to wrestle. He wanted us to save our energy for work. But we were out in the field, Mr. Stutzman was nowhere around, and there was nothing to do, so Whitey and I were soon rolling around the potato patch in a wrestling match.

Before we knew it there was the sound of an engine, a cloud of dust, the slam of a truck door and the shadow of Mr. Stutzman. As he pulled us apart he asked if we had heard him say "no wrestling." Both of us knew the rule.

All I could think of was, "I have lost my job. I'm fifteen years old and I've been fired." I also felt bad that I had disappointed him. He gave me a job. He paid me well. He picked me up every morning for work. He took me home every night. Often the Stutzmans invited all of us dirty teenagers to join them for lunch at their farmhouse table. Now I had disobeyed him and would never work for him again.

I prepared myself for the inevitable. "You broke the rule. I'll find some other boys to work for me who can keep the simple rules. You're through. Get your lunch bucket. You're going home. No need to come back tomorrow. I'll mail your check."

I didn't know how it would come, what words he would choose, how long he would delay in telling us, but I knew. We were through. I was fired.

Mr. Stutzman did give Whitey and me a lecture. Then he said, "Now get back to work. No more wrestling."

Get back to work?

I wasn't fired. I didn't have to tell my parents I was a failure. There would be a second chance. I could start over.

I Feel Like a Failure

This close call with losing my job reminded me of all my other childish failures. My mess-up in the potato patch made me think of fifth grade when I tried to learn to play the drums, but I couldn't keep the beat. In sixth grade I took guitar lessons at the music store above the Church of the Brethren where I had gone to Vacation Bible School, but I could only master two chords. I tried selling Christmas cards door-to-door, but my average pay was something like three cents per hour. In the vacant lot across the street from our home, I built a club house, but it kept falling down. When I helped my father brick the house, I often heard "the mud is too wet" or "the mud is too dry"–mason talk for "you failed to do it right."

I had an Ishmael complex: I was the other child, the one not chosen, the one cast out, the one most likely *not* to succeed. What could you say about a kid that couldn't even keep one rule in the potato patch?

Failure made quite an impression on my life. I was good at it, but I have discovered that most children feel the same isolation and rejection I felt because they don't seem to be good enough, don't make the team, or fail at what they try. That raises questions. Why do some kids seem doomed to failure? Why do adults put such pressure on kids to excel? Is there a place where the comparisons made by other kids don't matter at all? Is there a role for the child who is not a star? Who gives significance to the child that never makes the grade? How can any child succeed in our culture's competitive climate that guarantees almost universal failure?

Hear God's Heart

God deals with failure in a striking way. His attitude toward those who don't measure up is absolutely amazing. Just think about all the failure in Genesis. After every miscue, God permits a new start. If God canceled the earth the first time someone made a mistake, the Bible would have been three chapters long. In Genesis the new start always involves the birth of a child as if to say that children represent God's willingness to move beyond the failure, move past the insufficiencies, and provide a new start once again.

After Adam and Eve sin, the next announcement is that Eve is expecting Cain. After one brother kills another we might expect a diatribe about how bad things are, but instead we get a list of Cain's descendants. Even the bad line gets a new start. After the flood in which God takes drastic measures to deal with human failures, there is a genealogy of the three boys who survive the disaster. Lot is a total disappointment. Our last word about him is the torrid scene in which his line is perpetuated. Jacob deceives Isaac. Laban deceives Jacob. Next we read about the birth of thirteen children to carry on the likes of Jacob and Laban. Genesis 35 makes it strikingly real. Verse 22 tells of Reuben's sin of sleeping with his father's concubine. Verse 23 lists the sons of Jacob. After sin comes a fresh start. After someone fails, God sends a child that represents a new beginning. Given the amount of sin and failure described in Genesis, it's no wonder the book is filled with so many genealogies. The fact that the human race continues tells us something about the creator and sustainer of the whole process.

God Picks the Unlikely

In addition to the way God deals with failure, Genesis shows that God picks the most unlikely people to do the most amazing things. Genesis 10 lists the great nations of the ancient world. Israel is not on the list. When God wanted to pick a people to bless, he didn't tap the Egyptians or Babylonians. He didn't pick Nimrod to carry his blessing. The people of Babel whose engineers built the first skyscraper were not the ones God chose to engineer the salvation story.

He chose Abraham.

Who?

Abraham. His name is not mentioned in the non-biblical literature of the ancient world. He built no city, wrote no law, directed no great army, built no pyramids. Nimrod is mentioned, but not chosen. Shinar is listed, but not selected.

God didn't choose the Michael Jordans who played for the Cairo Pharaohs, or the Donald Trumps who developed housing on the Sea of Galilee, or the John Grishams who were writing up the Babylonian creation story. The one who got the call, who received the letter in the mail, was a childless man bent on obscurity.

After Abraham, God picked Isaac to carry on his line. Isaac hardly makes an impression on the biblical reader. At times the Genesis story seems to move from Abraham to Jacob, with Isaac as a blip on the screen. Somebody else buries his mother, picks his bride, decides on the birthright, and borrows his wife. His major role in the story comes when he fumbles the passing on of the blessing in Genesis 27. What God did with Isaac typifies what he did with others. When God chose Abraham he did it based not on Abraham's skills, but on God's blessing. Five times in the blessing in Genesis 12 God uses the pronoun I.

"*I* will make you into a great nation"

"*I* will bless you"

"*I* will make your name great"

"*I* will bless those who bless you"

". . . .whoever curses you *I* will curse"

I. I. I. I. I. Not Abram, not Isaac, but God.

God picks people not based on their potential, but on his potential; not based on their success, but on his; not based on their abilities, but on his abilities. Think of the people whose stories dominate Scripture. For the most part they didn't stand out in their own time. There are a few Samsons and Solomons, but mostly it's obscure men like Isaac, liars like Jacob, poor girls like Ruth, timid women like Esther, fishermen like Peter, and unmarried girls like Mary. In God's hands they become somebody.

It doesn't get any clearer than in the Ishmael story.

The Boy God Hears

On three occasions God steps into a messy situation to restart the boy's life. (1) In Genesis 16 Sarah gives Hagar to Abraham so that they can have the son that God promised. No sooner is Hagar pregnant than problems arise between the two women. Sarah sends

---

ଓ ଚ

This Child

Means the World

to God

Lydia lives in our neighborhood. Through a mutual friend we learned that she had quit eating and became obsessed with fat grams. She was afraid of not being the right size, of being different from the other students at school. The pressure to be perfect was more powerful than the hunger pains she denied.

the expectant mother to the wilderness. An angel of God tells her to go back home, but the unborn child is not overlooked. God promises to see that the child is born. (2) When Ishmael is thirteen, Abraham pleads his case before God, in effect asking that Ishmael be made the child of promise. God insists that Abraham and Sarah will have that promised child. But even as those words fall from heaven, they are followed by words about the one who is *not* the child of promise, the left out son.

> And as for Ishmael, I have heard you: I will surely bless
> him; I will make him fruitful and will greatly increase his
> numbers. He will be the father of twelve rulers, and I will
> make him into a great nation (Genesis 17:20).

Twice God turns aside to the child turned aside. The favored child will get his favor, but the unfavored child is not overlooked. (3) Then Abraham sends Hagar and fourteen-year-old Ishmael to the desert with a canteen of water. Hagar is determined to survive, but the boy seems doomed to die. Hagar deserts him. Ishmael cries under a bush. Ishmael. *God hears.* Then God speaks about the boy's future for the third time: "I will make him into a great nation" (Genesis 21:18). This time Ishmael's life is summarized as one under the protection of God himself.

> God was with the boy as he grew up. He lived in the
> desert and became an archer. While he was living in the
> Desert of Paran, his mother got a wife for him from Egypt
> (Genesis 21:20-21).

Ishmael's story reveals an insight about God who gives the runner-up a second and third chance. The other son is not forgotten. The one not chosen is not neglected.

Our competitive culture poses a challenge to all who care about children. By investigating the parallel lives of two brothers, Ishmael and Isaac, we learn about God's culture which allows each child a chance to achieve his potential. God had a plan which would permit each boy to become significant in his own way. In the power structures of the ancient world, neither brother was a king nor man of note. God chose Isaac to play a special role in his redemption story. That choice resulted in a rivalry between the two that allowed God to show that even the one not chosen for a special role could achieve his full potential in another significant way. God planned for each of the brothers to reach his potential, just as the father in the story of the prodigal son wanted each of his children to grow. That quality of God becomes a model for the Christian community which must provide a place for today's lonely and rejected children to be all they can be. All children, regardless of action or ability, mean the world to God.

Hear the Call

God created an alternative world for children who feel unforgiven and second best. He showed us that even those who don't get picked first can be people of significance in life. That says something important about the culture we create in our churches. In a world of three strikes and you're out, there must be a place where even after 490 strikes, you can still play. Children must learn about both sin and grace. To teach them only about sin is to fragment the gospel, to tell the story of Eden but not Calvary. The world has never been good at forgiveness. Only God excels in dispensing grace. Churches, through their modeling, preaching, teaching, literature, and unwritten rules, must keep the link between sin and grace.

Word that one of the teens at church had been arrested with an illegal substance spread quickly through our church community. We were all saddened, not only by the revelation at what was going on in his life, but at the jail sentence that would surely follow. What caught me by surprise was the response of the other teens and their parents. In one of our worship services, they gathered around him. Some people had to move so that the crush of teens and college students coming to support their wayward and now returning friend could express their solidarity by an expression of grace. More surprising was the number of Christians who attended the trial not to jeer, but cheer. One of the volunteer youth workers even agreed to pay for the young man's college tuition while he was out on bail to help him get a new start in life.

Such actions revealed that we had succeeded in conveying our God's sense of sin and grace. No one applauded his sin. But a host affirmed his forgiveness. It was a powerful message to our teenagers, but also a significant word to our younger children. Don't mess up. It's not worth it. But if you do mess up, you are still welcome here. This is the place to come to start over.

That kind of accepting climate reflects the culture of God. In our competitive world it is difficult to create an alternative society in our churches. The society so influences the church that we struggle to keep the vision of another paradigm alive. When we bring the competitive nature of society into the church, we create rivalry, we pit children in our own churches against each other. A child who feels inferior on the soccer field, or in the biology lab, must not feel second rate in God's house.

One way we perpetuate such feelings of inferiority is by creating a climate of perfectionism. We transfer the perfection of our God onto our children. Then when they can't measure up to our standards, they are overcome with feelings of unworthiness and failure. Rather than an environment of forgiveness and nurturing where they feel loved, this atmosphere of perfection stifles the ability of our children to grow spiritually because they can't survive in a climate where the goals are unattainable. This drives our children away. They need what we all need: a place to feel loved in spite of our flaws, forgiven in spite of our failures, and cherished because we are his children.

Accepting Second Stringers

We must learn to see the potential God has put in each child, not the potential we want to see in each child. We must create a place where anybody can try something new for them. Instead of honoring only the children who achieve greatness by the world's standards, we must create a place for each child to find significance. When the church imitates the secular culture in honoring only the winners, it creates in the spiritual community a rivalry between children which mirrors the world and not the God who found a place for both Isaac and Ishmael.

We must acknowledge the different ways children develop and the different levels they can ultimately achieve. God made us all different. We must not have the same expectations for all children any more than we have the same standards for all adults. Nobody expects the church counselor and the church janitor to have the same abilities, but we frequently have the same high, often unattainable, expectations of children.

God's attention to children reminds us to value each child by creating a place for them in the church. Handicapped children, young people who have special emotional problems, the physically unattractive and those who have other qualities that leave them rejected by the world must all be welcome and valued in the spiritual community. Both children and adults habitually form cliques that exclude the different or unwanted. Churches must teach and stress the need to resist such barriers and welcome all into our community just as God has welcomed us all into his.

The church must not only be a place of grace for the sinner, but a community that values those the world has decided are second best. The professional sports team doesn't want the second stringers, only the starters. The top accounting firms don't want those who eked through graduate school, they want the honor students. The world has a strict pecking order. Those at the bottom seldom get to the top.

A Different Standard

As a teenager I often felt like a failure and second best, but in the church community I found a different set of standards. A few months after my conversion the preacher asked me to do a talk on Wednesday night in front of the church. That was risky. I wasn't prepared for that at all. I made my way to his office after church to get some direction.

"How do you do a talk?" I asked.

He gave me some pointers. I worked hard on what I should say. Afterward all the people came up to tell me how much they enjoyed my message. I remember being amazed that adults would say that about the mumblings of an eighth-grade boy. Now I see what they were doing. It was another case of Abraham being asked to carry the blessing. Another Isaac or Ishmael moved to center stage.

Few people are as good at seeing the potential in others as my friend Gerald. I was his assistant coach when we worked with the fourth grade soccer team. Gerald was a wonderful coach. I learned more than the boys did. Gerald approached coaching like God approached the people in Genesis. He had a way of picking the most surprising boy to do the most outstanding work on the team. Fourth graders have a way of establishing the pecking order. Trey and Russ were team favorites. They knew it. The coaches knew it. The team knew it. If Trey and Russ played all the time we just had to win.

But Coach Gerald had another philosophy. The kid I would never have used was carefully developed into a suitable goalie despite the protests of Trey and Russ. Every boy played, but more significant was the fact that the boys who held back, who often missed the ball when they tried to kick it, who confused the rules of baseball and soccer, were the ones who experienced the most improvement. All of us felt great joy when one of the boys from whom nobody expected anything scored the last goal in the last minute of the last game.

Coach Gerald got his philosophy from God and he learned it in church. He learned it in a community that has set itself up as a counter culture. In a world that plays only the stars, the church plays the ones who trip over their own feet. In a world that favors only the pretty or the strong, the church values the plain and the weak.

The Challenge

Feelings of failure, inferiority, awkwardness and unworthiness often characterize childhood. God calls the church to hear these cries of children by being a community that values each child and provides an atmosphere where every little boy and girl can become the person God intended them to be. In that kind of setting, the church becomes the conduit through which God changes these youngsters. As they change, so does the entire world in which we live.

Everybody is Somebody

One Sunday service brought it home to me. The order of worship said I was next. With Bible in hand, my mind on the opening lines and the text to follow, I moved to the front. I heard my voice amplified by the microphone. The lesson was launched. About five minutes into my talk I happened to look at the one operating the public address system. Instead of the trusted adult with years of experience adjusting those knobs and pushing buttons, I saw an eighth grader. An alarm went off in my head. My lesson is in the hands of a fourteen-year-old! I quickly put the thought out of my mind, for to dwell on it would have made it impossible to finish my lesson.

Later that day I weighed the issue. Was it wise to have an eighth grader running sound? Were we not taking a chance that things would go wrong? Shouldn't we go with our first string? Let's use the best people for the task. Then it struck me. That wasn't the culture of our congregation. It was a place where you didn't have to be a star to be part of God's great story.

Exercises

Hear a Child

1. Tell about a child who needs a chance.

2. Tell about a child who needs a second chance.

3. Put an "X" on the line below that reflects how you felt about yourself as a child.

Successful_____Failure

Why did you feel that way? Now put an "O" on the line that reflects God's view of you. Why does he feel that way?

Hear God's Heart

4. Why do new babies give us such hope? When you think of genealogies as a list of new babies, what do they teach us?

5. To whom did God give a second chance in the Bible? How did he give them a second chance? What was the result?

Who   **How**   **Result**

6. Read 1 Corinthians 1:26-29. Give biblical examples of the kind of people suggested in this text. Give examples you see in your church.

Hear the Call

7. Think of a child that needs acceptance in your congregation. Make a list of actions you can take to encourage him or her and then follow through.

8. What part of your congregation's culture encourages and welcomes those that the world leaves out?

Chapter Ten
They Are All Our Children

Hear A Child

At the 1996 National Prayer Breakfast in Washington, D.C., the speaker told about an American reporter covering the conflict in Sarajevo who saw a little girl hit by a sniper bullet. The newsman threw down his pad and pencil, stopped being a reporter, and rushed toward the child. A local man arrived first and cradled her in his arms. The American helped them both into his car and sped to the hospital. Not far down the road the man holding the bleeding child said, "Hurry, my friend, my child is still alive."

A moment later he cried again, "Hurry, my friend, my child is still breathing."

Another block or two passed when the man pleaded a third time, "Hurry, my friend, my child is still warm." As they approached the hospital he called again, "Hurry, my child is getting cold."

They were too late.

Later the two men were in the bathroom washing the blood off their hands and clothes. The local man turned to the reporter. "This is a terrible task for me. I must tell her father that his child is dead. He will be heartbroken."

The reporter was amazed. He looked at the grieving man.

"I thought she was your child."

The man looked back. "No."

Then he added a line that I can't forget. The man who had cradled the hurting child, not his own, verbalized what motivated his action. The one who ventured onto the street where the sniper had just hit a small child gave insight into his courageous heart. "No, she is not my child." Then the line:

"Aren't they all our children?"

A man I will never know raised an issue that I can never forget. An action that I did not witness poses a question that I cannot neglect. A sad story about a terrible tragedy to a little girl who lived far away raises critical questions for all who follow Christ. Aren't they all our children?

We have learned to repress the stories of hurting children. There's too much to take in. We see terrible things done to children every day on television. We hear too much about people abusing children. I have no desire to add to your pain over such issues, but I must raise questions. I must inquire about what we should do. It will not do to turn away from such stories to avoid the reality of so much suffering as if we imagine that because their suffering is far away or repressed from our mind, that it matters less, or not at all.

All that we have studied together, all of the Scriptures that have surprised, comforted, or critiqued us, all of the emotions that we have felt on this brief journey will somehow be in vain if nothing changes in the way we do church. Tremendous barriers keep us from ministering to children in a fully biblical way. This chapter is a call to overcome those barriers and to find the will to help children.

Hear God's Heart

There are always reasons not to act. One day Jesus stepped off the boat onto the dock at Capernaum. One of the most important men in the city met him with a request. Jairus' child was dying. Would Jesus help? Jesus agreed to go.

On the way the two men encountered four barriers. First, the crowd decided to come along. The congestion slowed their travel. We can almost imagine the father begging Jesus, "Hurry, my child is still alive."

Second, an unnamed sick woman approached Jesus and he stopped to ask who it was that touched him. Jesus healed her and called her "daughter." Jairus must have been thinking, "Jesus, my child is still breathing."

Third, a servant came from the man's house announcing that the child had died and there was no need for Jesus to come. It's too late. The poor father must have thought, "Jesus, my child is

❧ ❧

These Children
Mean the World
to God

For the third time in two years, four of us from Memphis sat in Dr. Lydia Miskovick's office in a small children's hospital in central Ukraine. In the first days after the fall of communism, God opened the door for us to meet some of the medical professionals in this eastern European nation. Dr. Miskovick's deep interest in children and warm welcome created a bond between us. One of the results of the new openness was that Ukrainian physicians were learning about how the rest of the world did medicine. Now she was crying, not just because there were few medications for the sick children or because her physicians had not been paid in a month, but because of news from her chief surgeon. A three-year-old child was dying. A simple diagnostic tool available in most doctor's offices in the western world could save her life.

getting cold." Jesus ignored the servant's suggestion. "Do not fear, only believe."

The fourth barrier was a group of mourners at Jairus' house who gathered to grieve the loss of the child. They mocked Jesus in his heroic attempt to save the little girl. Despite the barriers, Jesus reached the child, called to her, and gave her back her life. She was an unknown child, in an unvisited place, belonging to an unfamiliar face. But Jesus sought her out, overcame the barriers, and renewed her life (Mark 5:21-43). Jesus' concern for this little girl reflects God's love for all children. From the dying child in Sarajevo to the one in Capernaum, children do mean the world to God.

The story reminds us of the power of one person to defeat the barriers and to help one child. The barriers Jesus faced are similar to ours. Often the barrier is a street in our own city.

96th Street

One barrier is 96th Street in New York City. Jonathan Kozol in his book, *Amazing Grace,* tells the story of children who live on both sides of that thoroughfare. It is a street that separates. He calls it the "demarcation line."

South of 96th Street in Manhattan, the average annual income is three hundred thousand dollars. The infant mortality rate is the lowest of any neighborhood on earth; just seven newborns die for every one thousand births. North of 96th Street, in one of the poorest and most unhealthy places in America, twenty-eight newborns die for every one thousand births, higher than many third world nations. The Number Six train makes only nine stops to move from the nation's wealthiest congressional district to the poorest.[13]

At one high school north of 96th Street, less than seventy of the seventeen hundred seniors qualified for graduation in the spring of 1994. Green fungus grows in the corners of the guidance counselor's office. Children must use the toilet at home because the school's restrooms are broken. Police patrol the streets around the school constantly to protect the students from crime. Graduates of another high school south of 96th Street earn more Ph.D.'s than those from any other secondary

---

[13]Jonathan Kozol, *Amazing Grace–The Lives of Children and the Conscience of a Nation* (New York: Crown Publishers, 1995), pp 3, 186-189.

school in the nation. The ten-story high school building, equipped with twelve science labs, five gyms, an Olympic-sized swimming pool, 450 personal computers, a forty thousand-volume library, and a "penthouse" cafeteria, caters to what the *New York Times* calls a "brainy bunch" that "deserves every bit of indulgence a cash-strapped city can muster."[14]

Two neighborhoods in the same city–separated. Two groups of children who speak the same language, are citizens of the same nation, and ride in the same subway cars–separated.

Jonathan Kozol's description of New York's 96th Street focuses on children. His book describes the desperate plight of poor American children, kids who live in New York and Nashville, from Mott Haven to Memphis. Especially poignant is his list of children in New York who died while he wrote *Amazing Grace*.[15] Kozol writes about New York City, but the application extends far beyond. Every city has its "demarcation line." New York has its 96th Street. Memphis has East Parkway. Milwaukee has the industrial valley. What is it in your city? The CSX tracks? The river? The freeway loop? A sports stadium? Somewhere in each community, there is an unofficial line that separates. On the other side of that line lies what the wealthy people call the "wrong" side of the tracks.

The world has its demarcation lines. The first world nations are separated from the third world countries. Children in totalitarian regimes are separated from those who live in freedom. Every day in the world 34,000 children die of starvation and easily-curable diseases. That's about one child every three seconds.

---

[14]Ibid., pp 152-154.
[15]Ibid., pp 253-256.

In one month enough children die to fill Memphis or Pittsburgh. The food we waste and the medicines we can purchase easily are separated from the children who need them most.

The Great Gulf

Jesus talked about barriers in the parable of the judgment in Matthew 25. He will separate all humanity, just as a shepherd divides the sheep from the goats. He forms two groups, one saved and one lost. The population of heaven is safely isolated from the fires of hell. The good separated from the bad. The "great gulf fixed" between the two eternal resting places will be the great spiritual "demarcation line."

In the same story where he mentions the eternal demarcation line, Jesus responds to those who fail to cross earthly demarcation lines: "Depart from me, you cursed, into the eternal fire prepared for the devil and his angels; for I was hungry and you gave me no food, I was thirsty and you gave me no drink, I was a stranger and you did not welcome me, naked and you did not clothe me, sick and in prison and you did not visit me" (Matthew 25:41-43, RSV).

Jesus knew about separation. He knew that the well-fed would be separated from the ill-fed. He knew about the barriers between the abundantly-clothed and the barely-clothed. He also knew about the "great gulf" that would be fixed for eternity. He knew about the divine sorting of sheep and goats. But most significantly, Jesus linked the two. If we do not want to be separated from God in the next world, we need to be connected to each other in this world. Theologically, the "great gulf" of Matthew 25 and 96th Street in New York City are intimately connected.

What is particularly striking about the parable is the move Jesus makes. He identifies himself with the people who are without. When the people asked Jesus, "Lord, when did we see thee hungry and feed thee, or thirsty and give thee drink? And when did we see thee a stranger and welcome thee, or naked and clothe thee? And when did we see thee sick or in prison and visit thee?" he answers, "Truly, I say to you, as you did it to one of the least of these my brethren, you did it to me" (Matthew 25:40, RSV).

"My *brethren*."

He doesn't say, our brethren or our church members. He doesn't say "when you did it to the least of these *your* brethren." Our brethren are the people at church. The ones with the asterisk beside their names in our church directory. They are the ones in our zone or small group. But Jesus defines *his* brethren as the people who are hungry and thirsty, homeless and naked, sick and imprisoned. Nothing about church directories, asterisks, or small groups.

The parable calls for us to break down the barriers that separate us from the people he wants us to help. Kozol merely describes the horrible conditions of American kids. Jesus offers solutions. Feeding the hungry means crossing the barriers. Jesus knew those lines existed, but he refused to leave them alone. "Cross them! Don't let the tracks separate. Don't allow the freeway to come between us. Cross those lines!"

The parable is about God's call to action, about how serving the weak and oppressed of society is doing something for God. He is God of the rich and poor, haves and have-nots, clean and dirty. It is a call for the people of God to have the vision of God.

The church must not limit its vision, hinder its dream, or restrict its ministry. We must be open to serving all the people God sends, all the people in every time and place that we can. It is a judgment day issue. It is a matter of spiritual life and death. They are all our children.

Hear the Call

Both Jesus' example in crossing barriers (Mark 5) and his teaching about what his followers will do for the disadvantaged (Matthew 25) call the church to action. We are surrounded by children in pain and suffering, neglected and abused, yet we often do not have the moral will to do anything about it.

These texts are a call to repent. Our inaction threatens the soul of the church. We deplete the life of the church by our inactivity. There are numerous obstacles to helping and taking action. The mandate from Jesus demands that we name those obstacles and overcome them. Whether it is fear of another part of town, our own selfish refusal to share the blessings God has given us, or the oceans that separate us from hurting children in third world countries, we must identify the source of our inaction and move to help.

It's Not a Lack of Money

One obstacle that many Christians bring up is the lack of resources. But to insist that we take no action because of resources is to insult God, who not only made everything, and owns everything, but promises us whatever we seek. We may be afraid to help children in our inner city, but it is not because of a lack of resources. We may not know how to help starving children in the third world, but there is enough food in the world to feed everybody. We may selfishly not care to give our time to children in the second world, but our failure to help children there is not because the means are lacking. Jesus reached the child because he had the will. Those he ushered into heaven were the ones who fed the hungry and clothed the naked. For Jesus it was not a question of resources, it was a question of the will. Are you willing?

The man was all excited. He lived in a public housing project next to the levee in West Memphis, Arkansas. He and his wife had just become Christians through a small ministry along Broadway, the city's main street. He cornered a volunteer in the storefront church building.

"Every piece. I've counted them all. All the kids. Me and the wife. All of us."

The volunteer tried to sort out what the man was saying. Was the family hungry? Did they miss their ride? Then the man got to the point.

"Every item of clothing our whole family is wearing came from this ministry."

Church members in affluent churches had gleaned through their closets to contribute to the inventory of a "Clothing Give Away." Poor children in America have clothing. That's not the problem. The problem is that they can't wash the clothes. This man's family lived in government housing. They had no washer and dryer. There was no Laundromat in the project. The nearest coin-operated washer was a mile away. They had no car. Public transportation was infrequent. Washing blue jeans and shirts in a tub and letting them dry on the railing was their only option, until a group of Christians provided them with an opportunity to shop for free.

"Every item of clothing our whole family is wearing came from this ministry."

Putting on a clothing give-away is not easy. It is filled with barriers. Some church members donate clothing that is unacceptable. Some sizes are in high demand and there are not enough to go around. Sorting clothing takes intensive volunteer time. Helping poor children is not a problem of resources. There are plenty of clothes. The key issue is, are we willing?

Not Resources but the Will

On a trip to Ukraine two of us visited a children's hospital in a village called Vascikov. We visited with the head physician, a delightful woman named Dr. Lydia Miskovick. She graciously offered us lunch, gave us gifts of local pottery, and invited us back. Six months later we visited again. Our determination to visit with her helped form a bond between us though we were separated by cultural and language barriers. In a moment of candor she told us that the Soviet government had lied to her. They assured her that her hospital was equipped as well as any in the world. But she couldn't understand why they could not help the children who were sick, especially the ones who were suffering the effects of radiation from the Chernobyl disaster. She learned that in other countries they had a non-invasive machine called an ultrasound that would put their diagnostic work ahead by years. But they had no money. Such machines were not even for sale in their nation.

We prayed. A local doctor heard about a Memphis hospital getting a new ultrasound. He inquired about the used one. They agreed to a small price, which they later waived. Northwest Airlines agreed to ship it free. A local doctor with expertise in ultrasound machines, a technician, and an engineer agreed to pay their own way to help deliver the machine and train the staff in Vascikov. With our ultrasound machine on the bus, we were met by the village mayor and a parade of local dignitaries and leaders. The ten thousand children of Vascikov now have an ultrasound. It was never a question of resources. It was always a matter of whether or not we were willing.

Do We Have the Will?

For years our family has corresponded with a young girl named Claudia who lives in the Dominican Republic. We have never met. Through the Christian Relief Fund (1-800-858-4038) in Amarillo, Texas, we deposit twenty-five dollars each month. Nearly all of that money goes to Claudia to help her family provide food and clothing for her. Because of our help she is going to school and doing well. Her letters are a delight to read. She and her family regularly attend church. We speak only English, Claudia speaks only Spanish. We have never been to her country, she has never traveled to ours. We live in different kinds of houses, exist in different cultures, and live radically different lives. Despite all those barriers, our twenty-five dollars and infrequent letters are making the difference in the life of one child. For us the twenty-five dollars was never a matter of resources. It has always been a matter of the will.

One day our teenage sons came home with exciting news. The entire youth group planned a fast. Through Manna International (1-800-253-2420) in Redlands, California, they had become part of an effort to drill a well in a rural African nation. The surface water in this village was impure, leading to many easily-preventable diseases. It would cost about ten thousand dollars to drill the well. Several youth groups around the nation joined the fast. They donated the money they would have spent on food to Manna, who sent the money to the well drillers. Now one village has clean water. Children who would have died of cholera, shigella, typhoid, and dysentery will now grow up healthy. It was never a matter of resources. It was always a matter of the will.

The Challenge

God has made our responsibility to children clear. He has put the resources at our disposal. He has shown us that by changing the lives of children, we play a critical role in altering the entire world. God has promised to work through the church. The question is, "Are we willing to be used by God?"

The two men in Sarajevo acted, but they were too late. The little girl died in a war she did not cause and probably never understood. If our teenagers had not fasted, children in an African village would have died. If our family had not been willing to part with twenty-five dollars a month, Claudia's life would be substantially different. If the Christians in Memphis had not given their unwanted clothing to a struggling inner city church in West Memphis, Arkansas, several families might have had no opportunity to come to Christ. Because of the work of medical people in Memphis, children in the far away agricultural town of Vascikov are living longer because of better and earlier diagnosis of their medical ills.

No church is too small or poor or remote to participate in God's plan to help needy children. Indeed the church that does not help will become small and mired in its own poverty of action and remote from the will of God. From Sarajevo to West Memphis, Arkansas, from that rural African village with the new well to the agricultural town of Vascikov with the new ultrasound machine, Christian people overcame barriers and changed the lives of children in significant ways. The barriers are always there. God refused to let them stand. The question is never resources, it is always the will.

After all, they are all our children.

Exercises

Hear A Child

1. What were your reactions to the story from Sarajevo?

2. Name a local barrier that separates you from children in your community.

Hear God's Heart

3. In Mark 5:21-43, why do you think Jesus continued in spite of the barriers he confronted?

4. In Matthew 25, Jesus mentions being hungry, thirsty, strangers, naked, sick, and in prison. How might children be included in each category?

Hear the Call

5. How do successful new ministries begin in your church?

6. Share an example of someone who has overcome barriers and served a need.

7. Reflect on Matthew 25. Discuss ways your church could help people with needs.

Chapter Eleven
The Right Thing

Hear A Child

Have you ever heard a story that bothered you, but you couldn't immediately put your finger on what was wrong, but then later, after some thought, the whole matter became clear? These three stories struck me that way.

The woman with three children in tow came by the church building asking for food. New to the congregation and untrained in such matters, I learned that one of the deacons usually handled these cases. He immediately began grilling the woman about her life, asking about her husband and the father of the children, inquiring about where she lived and the amount of her income. Each question was asked in such a way that it implied a negative judgment about the decisions she had made. After the questions were over, he made his decision. She passed.

"She can have one bag of groceries."

Maybe it was her hunger, or the constant demands of the children, or the deacon's interrogation, but she started to cry. The deacon seemed to enter the tears into the equation.

"Give her two bags, but no more."

We got the keys to the benevolence room, worked our way through the locks to the food that had been donated. She quickly did her shopping and went on her way.

After witnessing the above events, a friend of mine told me a second story. She remembers that a family in her childhood congregation brought a disabled child to church. After a couple of weeks, there were three other children in wheelchairs that joined the first. They made a row of worshipers where there had been none before.

Two months later members complained to the elders. Some murmurings were more polite than others, but it boiled down to one issue: "These handicapped children disturb our worship." The elders met, called in the family responsible and told them they could no longer bring these special children to church. They were out.

One day in a Memphis hospital, I met Ann, who told me the third story. She lived in a nearby city where a large population of Asian immigrants had settled. Several women in the congregation joined Ann to begin a ministry to those Asian children. Soon nearly a hundred Asian children were being served and taught about Jesus. A visitor to the large, mostly white congregation would immediately notice the Asian presence.

Two months later members complained to the church leaders. Some murmurings were more polite than others, but it boiled down to one issue: "These Asian children are overrunning our church." The leaders met, called in the women and stopped the church's outreach to Asian children. The ministry was off. The children were out.

It's Not Right

Something strikes me as wrong about all three stories. It's not the way God's people should be. There is something wrongheaded, something not fair. If Ishmael had died under that tree, the Bible might be a different book, but God heard. He heard the cry of a child that was being denied what was right. God heard and acted. If the father had quizzed the prodigal son about his behavior, wrinkled his brow, and then said, "He can stay for two days," we would be led in a different direction. But the father embraced the son and welcomed him home.

Treating other people unfairly has a long history. Hurting children is part of that notorious legacy. In the last quarter of the twentieth century Americans killed thirty-one million unborn children. At the beginning of the twenty-first century more than thirty-four thousand children around the world die every day from starvation and easily-curable childhood diseases. Add to those numbers the children abused and shot and left alone. Something is terribly wrong.

All of this unfairness toward children raises haunting questions. If we help just one hurting child, do we really make a difference in the statistics? What can we do in the face of such insurmountable forces? Why do some children enjoy good things and others suffer? Can we ignore the suffering of children we do not know as long as we care for those we do know?

Hear God's Heart

God has not left us alone on this important issue. The ultimate response to all these questions is the biblical doctrine of justice. From cover to cover the Bible speaks about justice and injustice, about fairness and oppression. From the call to Abraham to direct his children in what is just and fair to James' demand to treat the poor visitor with kindness and the warning to the rich, God speaks about fairness. But no part of Scripture addresses it with the power and clarity of the prophets. Isaiah, Hosea, Micah, and Amos all champion this issue. Perhaps one of the best known Old Testament passages is found in the wonderful words from Micah: "And what does the LORD require of you? To act justly and to love mercy and to walk humbly with your God" (6:8). Behind those wonderful words is a strikingly powerful context. What Micah does in his opening chapters is threefold: (1) He describes an ancient unfairness toward children; (2) He tells us God's response; (3) He shows us how to respond to that unfairness.

Unfairness Toward Children

Micah describes injustice in ancient Jerusalem:

> Woe to those who plan iniquity, to those who plot evil on their beds! At morning's light they carry it out because it is in their power to do it. They covet fields and seize them, and houses, and take them. They defraud a

man of his home, a fellow man of his inheritance. (Micah 2:1-2)

The people in Jerusalem were staying awake at night thinking up ways to oppress people. The lights in their houses were not for people praying, but for people plotting; not for folks reading Torah, but for planning terror; not for worshipers home late from the temple, but for people staying up late to prepare for torture. When the morning came, they carried out their plans: The people in power took away the lands and homes of others.

Some think that the rich landowners were taking or buying up the land of the small farmers in the same way that Ahab took Naboth's vineyard. A small farm might be worth ten thousand dollars, but they would force a farmer to sell for a hundred. A family would wake up one morning with a small flock of sheep and a tiny garden, but by dinner time they had lost their land and were pulling a cart down the street looking for a place to sleep.

Others think that these plotters were taking advantage of the aftermath of war. Judah had fought several wars in which a large number of men had been killed or were made prisoners of war (2 Kings 16:5; 2 Chronicles 28:5-19). These plotters grabbed up the land of the unsuspecting and unprepared war widows. Wounded soldiers came back from battle and couldn't defend their homes. These ruthless people just kicked them out on the street.

Micah 2:9 explains more about the situation:

You drive the women of my people from their pleasant homes. You take away my blessing from their children forever.

These greedy people drove women out of their houses and took the blessing away from the children. The "blessing" (some translations have "glory") means their inheritance. Robbed of their only resources, these children would grow up in poverty, with little hope.

God's Response

The next text is rated R for violence. I wish it weren't there. I'd rather not read it again. I don't like to explain this verse. But it is there. It is the Word of God:

> Then I said, "Listen, you leaders of Jacob, you rulers of the house of Israel. Should you not know justice, you who hate good and love evil; who tear the skin from my people and the flesh from their bones; who eat my people's flesh, strip off their skin and break their bones in pieces; who chop them up like meat for the pan, like flesh for the pot?" (Micah 3:1-3)

The sounds of Micah are not pretty. We hear the pain of people having their skin torn from their bodies. The cries of those being boiled for the enjoyment of others, the sound of a heavy knife cutting through human flesh, and the cracking of femurs and ribs echo offensively in our ears.

I want to say, "Stop it. Stop it. Tell Micah to be quiet. Take this book out of the Bible. Let's move on to something else." God speaks in return. "Turn up the volume. Take your hands off your ears. Listen to the sounds. Listen to my prophet. Listen to the sounds of evil."

When people don't treat others fairly, when they oppress those around them, God Almighty compares it to cannibalism.

When people stay up at night thinking of new ways to oppress others, God says that it is like eating people. When people rationalize their acts as being okay which are in reality unfair, God pulls out the stops and uses a revolting image to shock us into his reality.

But there's another shocking aspect of this text. The people practicing this unfairness were *God's people*. Micah 2-3 is not about the cruel Assyrians, or the bloodthirsty Philistines, or the warlike nations of the ancient world who impaled their captives, murdered their kings and offered their children on altars. These people lived in Jerusalem, read the Torah, went to temple, prayed for the Messiah, preached about mercy, and in the words of Micah, ate children.

Hear the Call

There is another sound from Micah, aside from the anguish of the unfairly treated women and children, and it comes in chapter one:

> Because of this I will weep and wail; I will go about
> barefoot and naked. I will howl like a jackal and moan
> like an owl (Micah 1:8).

It's not just the weeping of the children we hear. It is the crying of Micah. It's not just the wailing of the mother whose child is now homeless, but the wailing of God's preacher. It's not just the children of Jerusalem who are shoeless, but Micah who goes barefoot. Not only are the women stripped of their clothes, but Micah preaches without suit or tie. Micah carries the banner of justice.

In a world with a long history of injustice and oppression, in a time when thousands of children die without the bare essentials of life, in a culture driven by consumerism and self-centeredness, there must be someone who carries the banner of fairness and justice, who demands that people be treated fairly, that children be raised with justice.

Raising the Banner

Micah did not stop all the world's injustice, but he raised the banner. We cannot stop all the unfairness around us, but we can be known as people who stand for what is right and fair, and who seek to treat people with dignity and honor, despite their situation.

We need not preach naked like Micah. We probably don't need to use his cannibal metaphor. We certainly don't want to howl like jackals. But we do need to stand for the right. Four observations from the Micah story will help us raise the banner.

(1) **We are often unaware of injustice.** Micah not only critiques the people for their injustice, he has to tell them they are doing it, reminding us that it is possible to live in such isolation that we are unaware of the injustice being done. If we live in that kind of ignorance, we have no way of knowing whether we are doing injustice ourselves. Micah calls us to be aware of what's going on around us.

(2) **Nobody is immune from doing injustice.** We read Micah with pain not only because women and children are being tragically abused, but because it is God's own people doing the abusing. One of the amazing issues in the eighth century prophets is that God must send a preacher to his own people to

point out the unfair ways they are treating their own populace. Micah calls us to be aware of our own injustice.

(3) *Carrying the banner of justice can make a difference.* Who would have thought that one prophet could stir up so much concern about unfairness. Although Micah may have believed that he would only touch a few people doing wrong things in ancient Jerusalem, his book has lived for nearly three thousand years and has urged thousands to live in a different way. Doing right, no matter how small, is always God's way. Some injustices are so ingrained in our culture that it will take more than one person to bring about change, but every person can contribute in some way to a fairer world.

(4) *Doing nothing about injustice runs counter to God's will.* Micah's great conclusion is succinctly stated. What does God require of us: Do justice. Do kindness. Walk humbly. God, through Micah, puts justice at the center of a life lived for God.

What do these principles look like in our world? How can we do our small piece to make the world more fair? As I think back to the day the deacon made the poor woman cry, or to my friend's report on how the elders told the disabled children they could not worship in their church, or to the leaders that stopped a ministry to Asian children, I think about others who have stepped forward to do the right thing. Two of those people are Trace and Mary and the justice they gave to April.

April and Sharon

When April was born, her mother, Sharon, was suffering from fifteen years of abusing drugs and alcohol. She worked as a prostitute to support her habits. April's older siblings lived with various family members. April never knew her dad. No sooner was April brought into the world than Sharon was taken to prison. The State became mother and father to baby April. Sharon made calls from prison to find out where April was living, who was taking care of her, and when she would get her back, but the calls were never returned.

It was not Sharon's first time in jail, but it would be her last. She found a post card in the trash that offered a Bible study course by mail. She signed up. She studied. She learned about God. She fell on the concrete prison floor and prayed to God. When she got out of prison she was baptized and started attending church. Someone there told her about HopeWorks, a life skills ministry of churches in Memphis that offers a thirteen-week period of full-time study to learn job-finding and -keeping skills. Seventy percent of the graduates support themselves completely. Sharon signed up, graduated, and got back on her feet.

Then April came home. Through HopeWorks, Sharon and April started attending the congregation where I am a minister. One spring day Sharon and April were in the women's restroom just before services. Sharon was prodding eight-year-old April to hurry up so they could get a seat before services began. Then Sharon and April heard a voice.

"I was April's foster mother."

It was Mary. She and her husband Trace had volunteered to be foster parents to April when Sharon went off to prison. They had kept April for several months. Sharon had tried to find out who was keeping April, but no one returned her calls. There in the restroom, two women who had never met fell into each other's arms.

Trace and Mary had April and Sharon over for dinner. They looked through the photo album at April's baby pictures. Sharon saw April's crib and visited her infancy bedroom. That evening Sharon caught up on what she had missed.

Being Fair in an Unfair World

April had been caught in the midst of tremendous evil and injustice. The people in her life had not been fair with her. But in the midst of that unfairness came two people who wanted to make things right, who were prepared to change diapers, wipe a runny nose, and mix formula for a child who was not their own, who would not live with them long, who might face even greater injustice in the future. They wiped away all the tears from her eyes. While April was at their house there was no more death, no sorrow or crying or pain. It was not heaven by any means, but it was God working through his people to do the right thing for a child who had been wronged.

But God worked far beyond what any participant in the story expected. No one expected the card in the trash, or the Bible study by mail, or the HopeWorks experience. Nobody expected the church April attended as a foster child to be the same one to which her mother would take her five years later. In a world filled with unfairness, April found justice.

Micah would have smiled at this story. He had seen so much injustice. He had witnessed so many children being deprived and cheated. He had cried so many tears over the unfair way others had been treated. To hear the story of Trace and Mary and Sharon and April would have made him purr like a kitten instead of howling like a jackal.

Not everybody can do what Trace and Mary did, but each Christian and every congregation can carry the banner of fairness that Micah modeled in his life. It might be as simple as devoting a Sunday night service to praying for hurting children. Children throughout the world face desperate situations. A quick call to an area Christian child care agency (see the appendix), to Manna International (1-800-253-2420), or to Christian Relief Fund (1-800-858-4038) can provide ample prayer requests for hurting children locally and around the world. Pray for the congregation's children and for all the people in the community who have a part in raising them. Pray for special events that focus on children, including Vacation Bible School and Sunday school, and for Christian child care organizations the church supports.

> ෪ ෨
>
> ### *This Child Means the World to God*
>
> *At a carpet factory in Cairo, Egypt, I watched a twelve-year-old girl run a weaving machine. While her supervisor turned his back, she held out her hand for a tip from us tourists. As she did the rough edge of the yarn nicked her finger. She stuck it in her mouth to hide the blood. The whole situation made me sad and angry. All I could think of was the contrast between my twelve-year-old son and this child.*

Most communities have several categories of at-risk children. Abuse hot lines, juvenile courts, child care agencies, and the Department of Human Services are usually willing to share information. Books such as Jonathan Kozol's *Amazing Grace* take an in-depth look at oppressed children in America. A prayer list might include the need for more foster parents, or a way to combat the increase in teen pregnancy, or a plan to eliminate drug sales to children. Decide how to distribute the list. Perhaps it could be printed on a refrigerator magnet as a reminder to pray about it at supper each day. Members will talk for months about the night they really prayed for children.

Identify Community Concerns

Beyond the night of prayer, the church could identify members who are nurses, teachers, social workers, and daycare workers. Call them together. Ask them how the church could reach out to children in the surrounding community. One church offers free babysitting on Friday night to parents of disabled and special children. Once a month they offer a support group for the parents to discuss their mutual concerns. The program calls for almost no budget and makes use of the church building at an otherwise unoccupied time.

Another local way to urge fairness for children is to support the area school teachers. Teachers devote their lives to kids. Leading a classroom of youngsters can be a difficult task in many American communities. Teachers often find themselves caught between demanding administrators, angry parents, and dissatisfied taxpayers. Yet they do a great deal to "train up a child." Some churches have centered an entire service around local teachers. Send somebody from the church to local schools to plan the event. Reserve a special section of the auditorium for them. Give each a flower. Ask the preacher to speak about the role of teachers. Challenge the teachers to pass on good values to the children. Pray for the teachers. Plan a receiving line or a fellowship meal afterward.

Most public schools appreciate community support. Formulate a plan with local school officials for how your church can help. For example, schedule a "school store" on a Saturday in August when needy children could come to the church basement or fellowship hall to "shop" for their needs. Ask school officials what supplies are needed. Collect boxes of crayons, paper, and pencils for free distribution. Train the church members to be gracious clerks and generous helpers. Serve cookies and punch. In the publicity, make it clear that each child must be accompanied by an adult.

Another simple idea to carry the banner for fairness involves inviting a representative of a child care agency or orphans' home to speak. Build the service around the critical text of James 1:27. Ask the director to tell the stories of the children they serve. Encourage him to ask one of their foster parents or adoptive fathers to come to share in the service. Focus the service on how Christians can help children. Spell out the steps it takes to be a foster parent.

A more significant plan is to interview parents who are struggling economically about what the church could do for their children. These discussions might open a whole new area of ministry. Ask the parents how the church could help.

The Challenge

The call to hear the cry of children is rooted in the fairness and justice of God. Children are so important to God that he calls the world to do justice. When God's people rise up to treat children with equity, those young people are transformed by the power of God. By bringing justice to one child, we begin a series of events that promotes fairness beyond our dream, bringing a higher standard to the entire world.

Being known as the church in the community that cares for children could be the best outreach strategy of our time. It also makes us more like Jesus who called the little children in his day to "come unto me." Whenever we do what is right, we join with great leaders like Micah who stand for justice in an unfair world. It's not easy for people like Trace and Mary to respond to a crisis in a baby's life. It's not easy for a church to create an environment in which Christians like Trace and Mary respond in fairness. Every Sunday when I stand up to preach I see Trace and Mary in one pew and then Sharon and April in another. Sometimes I smile, thinking about what God did through his people and how one little part of the world is a better place because somebody made the effort to do the right thing.

Exercises

Hear A Child

1. Give examples of how children in today's world are treated unfairly.

2. Talk about a time when you were treated unfairly. How would a child handle those feelings?

Hear God's Heart

3. Read the entire book of Micah and make a list of the injustices he mentions.

4. Discuss Micah 6:8. List ways his call can be lived out today.

Hear the Call

5. After reading the ministry suggestions at the end of the chapter, add to the list. Form a task force to research the most likely ministries and make suggestions.

6. Share examples of people stepping forward to do what is right. Take time to pray and thank God for them.

7. Follow through on one of the suggestions below:

    ◆   Devote a Sunday night service to praying for hurting children.

    ◆   Call a Christian Child Care Agency, Manna International, 1-800-253-2420 or Christian Relief Fund, 1-800-858-4035, to get names and prayer requests for children in need.

    ◆   Pray for all your Sunday school teachers by name.

- Pray for families that have adopted or are fostering children.

- Offer to care for a special needs child to give the parents a night off.

Chapter Twelve
Major in Mercy

Hear A Child

On the way back from a campaign in Ukraine we were going to stop in St. Petersburg. Before we left Kiev, we had dinner with Ludmilyah. This kind Ukrainian woman gave us a package of candy and said the children in St. Petersburg didn't have any sweets.

"Give this candy to them."

One of the places we visited in St. Petersburg was Isaac's Cathedral, built in honor of Ishmael's younger half-brother. Inside the huge empty building our group sang "Amazing Grace." Acoustics were near-perfect and our little group sounded like a chorus of angels. Outside we ran into a group of Russian children on a school field trip. They were cute and pretty. My wife, Sally, got out the bag of candy to distribute to the children. Anxious to get their sweets, they crowded around, but they were all polite and said "Spasibo," the Russian word for "Thank you."

A few minutes later it was time to get back on the bus. As we loaded, a group of beggar children surrounded us. A dirty little boy about ten years old with an even dirtier baby on his back approached Sally and me. We had on winter coats. He just had a sweater. The baby was wrapped in an old rag. Their faces were smudged. He held his hands out. I ignored him.

After I got on the bus, he found the window where I was sitting, pressed his nose against the glass and held out his hand. I rigidly faced forward refusing to acknowledge his presence. Finally the bus lurched forward and I could relax. But as the boy fell to the side, a painful thought fell into my heart. The words I had sung started to mock me.

Amazing grace! How sweet the sound! That saved a wretch like me!

I once was lost, but now I'm found; Was blind, but now I see.

I had celebrated the amazing grace for my own lostness, but then sang a different song about the lost beggar boy I encountered. I had stood in amazement at God finding me, only to be selective about the people I served. I recognized my own wretchedness, but then could not recognize another because of his wretchedness.

My behavior prompted questions. Why was it so easy to give candy to the shiny-faced children who politely waited their turn, and so hard to give even a look of recognition to the dirty-faced child who insistently pursued me to my seat? Why is mercy easier to do when the recipient is clean?

Then I started to think about mercy beyond the parking lot of St. Isaac's. What prompts a person to show mercy to a child? Do lonely children find mercy and kindness in our congregation? If not, how could we change that? What children need our love? How do we find them? I found the answers to these questions sooner than I ever expected.

Amazing Grace

The next day at a St. Petersburg museum I saw a picture of a good father and a bad son that at first glance reminded me of the difference between the beggar boy and me. The father was nicely dressed, the son in rags. The father was fully attired, the son barely covered. The father had the means, the son begged for help. Yet the father in the picture did what I failed to do in the parking lot. He showed mercy.

First, it was the echo of John Newton's song that we sang in St. Isaac's that cri-

---

∓ ∞

This Child Means the World to God

As we sat in the lounge of the Kiev Children's Hospital, I listened to the 23-year-old mother tell of holding her six-month-old child. The little girl would not stop crying. The nurses and doctors provided warm, moist cloths, and rubbed the baby's back, but they could do nothing more. The baby had a simple infection. There were no antibiotics available. The child was going to die.

tiqued my actions. Now it was Rembrandt's "The Return of the Prodigal Son." As we passed through the Hermitage Museum, I remember staring at that painting. I didn't know it then, but I was beginning a long journey, a journey back to Luke 15, a trip into the heart of God. John Newton had made the same trip. "I once was lost, but now I'm found" comes from Jesus' story of the father and two sons.

Hear God's Heart

The setting of the story is particularly important. In Luke 15:1 the tax collectors and sinners gathered around Jesus much like those beggar kids surrounded me at St. Isaac's parking lot. The rejects of society wanted to hear Jesus. It must have been a wonderful scene. People were flowing in from all sides to hear the master. Then comes verse 2.

The religious people didn't like verse 1. They murmured something unpleasant about the unpleasant people Jesus associated with. They didn't like dirt. They didn't like the riffraff Jesus collected. When Jesus saw what was happening, he told three stories, one about a lost sheep, another about a missing coin, and the final one about a prodigal son. The last story is more about the father than the son.

Perhaps there is no verse in the Bible that tells us more about God than Luke 15:20:

So he got up and went to his father. But while he was still a long way off, his father saw him and was filled with compassion for him; he ran to his son, threw his arms around him and kissed him.

It tells us God is waiting for the lost sinner, that God has compassion for hurting people, that God is running toward us to meet us, that he is waiting to pull us into his arms, that he is willing to give us the kiss of grace.

Listen to the Heartbeat

Of all the scenes in this story that Rembrandt could have painted, he chose just one moment. He could have drawn the boy leaving home or captured the time when he comes to his senses in the pig pen or pictured the great party or exposed the older brother. None of that. Rembrandt captures verse 20. Not all of the verse, but just one part. Not the boy getting up to go home, nor the father waiting, or the old man running. But the last line when he threw his arms around him and kissed him.

Rembrandt helps us to see visually what this text says verbally. Rembrandt's father is bent over, hands on the back of his returning son; the boy is on his knees, his head dirty, his clothes torn, one sandal ripped, the other missing. But what particularly strikes me about the painting is the boy's head. The head of the son rests on the father's chest, left ear against his dad's shirt in the hollow spot above the abdomen. The boy's left ear is tight against his father's chest.

What is Rembrandt saying? Why this pose? Why this moment? Then I saw what the son heard. The prodigal heard the father's heartbeat. His left ear against his chest. Hearing the pounding, hearing the beating, hearing the music of his father's heart. The prodigal heard what John Newton later verbalized:

Amazing grace! How sweet the sound! That saved a wretch like me!

I once was lost, but now I'm found; Was blind, but
now I see.

God's wonderful grace is lived out in the compassionate heart
of the wounded father who welcomes his offending son back
home. As the son listened to the beating of his father's heart, he
sensed the welcome and acceptance that resulted from mercy.
Through the father's compassion toward the son, God models
mercy to all. God cares about the urchin who begs from tourists
in St. Petersburg. God cares about the loud little boy in your
neighborhood who has never been to church. God cares about
all the lost sons who are far from home.

The Sound of Mercy

When we are close to God, close enough to hear his heartbeat,
what we hear is mercy. When as the prodigal son we come to
God, it is mercy that we receive. Every time we think through this
story, it is mercy that shines most brightly. God reaches out to
those who are lost, neglected, rejected, lonely, sinful, and isolated and draws them home with his mercy. What we cannot miss
in the story is that the adult father extends it to a child. The same
God who heard Ishmael hears the prodigal and creates for us a
model of how we must respond to the world's lonely children.
Children mean the world to God because he is filled with mercy.

How could I read Scripture, get a graduate degree in biblical
studies, and miss this critical element? Jesus told two parables
that have caught the attention of people in all ages: the good
Samaritan in Luke 10 and the prodigal son in Luke 15. Both stories focus on the centrality of mercy. At the high point of his sermon on the plain in Luke 6:36, Jesus says, "Be merciful, just as

your Father is merciful." When the people didn't understand his ministry, he told them: "But go and learn what this means: 'I desire mercy, not sacrifice'" (Matthew 9:13).

Jesus obviously knew about the two texts widely regarded as the twin peaks of Old Testament prophecy. Hosea 6:6 says, "For I desire mercy, not sacrifice." Micah 6:8 elaborates a bit more: "He has showed you, O man, what is good. And what does the LORD require of you? To act justly and to love mercy and to walk humbly with your God." No wonder Jesus lectured the Pharisees about majoring on minors and minoring on majors:

> Woe to you, teachers of the law and Pharisees, you hypocrites! You give a tenth of your spices—mint, dill and cummin. But you have neglected the more important matters of the law—justice, mercy and faithfulness. You should have practiced the latter, without neglecting the former. (Matthew 23:23).

Somehow in my study I had neglected the same things the Pharisees had neglected. The message of Hosea and Micah fit me as well as the eighth century Israelites. Showing mercy is a hard lesson to learn.

Hear the Call

Justice, which we discussed in the last chapter, joins hands with mercy. Justice provides the standard. Mercy adds the concern. Calling for the right thing makes the world more fair. Doing the merciful thing makes the world more livable. We join Micah in *calling* for justice. We join Jesus in *doing* mercy. The banner of mercy is carried by people who practice it. Our churches can best advocate for mercy by being a merciful community.

In *The Jesus I Never Knew*, Philip Yancey tells of talking with a friend in Chicago who worked among the poor. The friend told of a prostitute who came seeking help. Her health was failing. She was homeless and desperate. She had no money to care for her two-year-old daughter so she started renting the little girl out. When Yancey's friend heard her story, he asked her if she had ever thought of going to a church for help. She looked at him with astonishment.

"Church! Why would I ever go there? They'd just make me feel even worse than I already do."[16]

Then Yancey asks a series of questions. Why do the poor who flocked to Jesus no longer feel welcomed by the people who now follow Jesus? Why do people like that Chicago woman think of the church as the last place to go?

I know the answer to those questions. Yancey never puts it in his book. He only raises the questions for us. But for me the answer is quite clear. People like the woman in Yancey's book don't go to churches because of people like me. I have a hard-hearted attitude toward the down-and-out. I am the toe-the-line person. Meet my standards. Keep my timetable. Do what I think is right.

Through the teaching of Luke 15 I have learned that I am called to show mercy. I don't do it naturally. I don't do it easily. No bell goes off inside me that says, "Be merciful as your father

---

16Philip Yancey, *The Jesus I Never Knew* (Grand Rapids, MI: Zondervan, 1995), pp 147-148.

is merciful." Learning to show mercy has been one of the hardest lessons I've ever had to learn.

Most of my life I have believed most of the stereotypes about the poor. Poor girls had babies to get more welfare money. Poor people were lazy. We should not help those who do not help themselves. Cleanliness is next to godliness. In short, I knew little about mercy.

When I take those spiritual gift tests, my lowest score is mercy. I'm great about passing by on the other side. I am more likely to be the priest or Levite than the good Samaritan. I more easily fit the role of the older brother than the father.

Then through this story in Luke 15 about a father and two sons I learned I had been wrong. Wrong about poor children. Wrong about mercy. Wrong about toeing the line. Wrong about the beggar boy in the parking lot.

All around us children are in trouble. Some are dying because they don't have simple antibiotics. Others are isolated from caring adults. Many are just confused. They are unwelcome in churches. They do not know God. They are crying out. They want someone to hear their cries.

Only one thing will make us respond when the children are dirty and different and destructive. Only one thing can take our hard hearts and closed fists and make us kind and generous. Only one thing can divert us from our quest to buy more, to please ourselves, to pad our pockets, to fortify our castles. Only one thing can ultimately make us into God's people: it is when we place our head against the chest of God and hear his heartbeat.

God illustrates what mercy looks like on a dusty road outside the family house when the prodigal comes dragging home. Let me offer several other things I've learned about mercy as God is delivering me from my own stubbornness and self-centeredness. Three things come to mind. (1) Mercy unites all people; (2) Mercy is aggressive; (3) Mercy saves lives.

Mercy Unites

Mercy is an interesting commodity in our divided world. We agree on few things in modern society. Multi-culturalism and tossed-salad societies breed diversity. Our world is so divided that there are few things about which most people agree. One is mercy. Regardless of race, national origin, education, or economic background, all people love mercy. Even stuffy people like me recognize and admire mercy when we see it, though we may have a difficult time showing it.

The media love mercy. The local television stations and newspapers love mercy. When our church has its annual school store, cameras and reporters from several media groups will be there to cover it. Hollywood loves mercy. A movie about a doctor who saves lives, or a rich man who rescues people from Nazi concentration camps, or a man who runs into a fire to save a neighbor, all make box office hits. Schools delight in students who take up projects of compassion, honoring such individuals before the entire student body. Government disaster aid and rescue operations are rooted in mercy.

There are no laws against showing mercy. Mercy is permitted in public places and in public schools. No one cries out discrimination when somebody shows mercy. Nobody says "I don't understand that language," because mercy is a universal language.

Mercy is Aggressive

Lydell Thomas leads a large inner city ministry in Nashville. He taught me about "aggressive mercy." Often we wait for people to come to us. Begging destroys dignity. People who ask for a handout must submit to our tests of efficiency before we will engage mercy. Lydell urges us to be more aggressive in showing mercy. He told about a young mother and her children who attended church one Sunday for the first time. A visitation worker called on the family the next day. The worker noticed the woman and her children had no furniture and passed the word on to a minister who dropped by later to confirm the report. While there, the minister asked the young mother a question.

"Would you mind if we brought a couch, a couple of chairs, and a bed over to your apartment? We can have the truck stop by tomorrow if it is convenient."

The young mother and her kids stared in disbelief. Pure mercy is a rare commodity. After saying "yes," questions started coming to their mind. Who are these people? Why do they care? Why are there no strings? Why is there no interrogation? They went back to church and came to know God.

We need aggressive mercy. We must be looking for children in need and finding ways to serve them, not waiting for them to come to us. We should be seeking them out, standing at the gate looking down the road to see if there is someone we can share our compassion with today.

Mercy Saves Lives

One of the repercussions of the fall of the Iron Curtain was the shortage of pharmaceuticals in Ukraine. The four children's hospitals we visited had empty medicine cabinets. The principal of a school that served children who had various cancers and diseases as a result of the Chernobyl nuclear disaster showed us his empty medical room. As we became aware of this need, we started taking children's aspirin and simple antibiotics to the physicians we had encountered. Then came the fall of 1994. Two of us sat in a children's hospital with three mothers from Kiev. They had no money and no jobs. All had recently borne children. Each told the story of how the life of their child had been threatened in childbirth or with a newborn ailment and how they had received antibiotics that we had carried to Ukraine in our suitcases. The cost had been about $3.50 per mother. Each mother had tears in her eyes as she thanked us for saving the life of her baby. Christians in Memphis showed mercy. Mothers in Kiev cried. Three children survived to grow up healthy.

But I Don't Know Any Children Who Need Mercy

One response we have to showing mercy is to say, "I don't know anybody who needs mercy." It's an old comment and it has an old answer. A lawyer asked Jesus about the great commandments. After a short discussion they settled on two commandments about love; that is, about mercy. Then the lawyer wanted to know, "And who is my neighbor?" Jesus told the story of the good Samaritan.

When Jesus finished his story, he turned to the man in the pin-striped suit: "Which of these three do you think was a neighbor to the man who fell into the hands of robbers?"

He said, "The one who had mercy on him."

Jesus responded, "Go and do likewise."

Jesus could have used any number of stories from our society.

An abandoned baby with genetic deformity arrived at the child welfare holding center. That afternoon three people passed by her crib. The first was. . . .

A five-year-old visited church with her aunt. Neither of her divorced parents gave her much affection. Starved for love, she entered a Bible class for the first time. The teacher. . . .

Two preteen sisters of an alcoholic mother needed a foster home. The case worker at the Christian child care agency called three churches to see if they had any foster parents. The people at the first church said. . . .

While the specifics differ, Jesus' point to the Jerusalem lawyer remains valid. People hurt as much in our day as they did in his. Our neighbors are still the ones who need our help.

Jesus tells us the first step in showing mercy: "Go." People don't come to us. Most of the children I meet when I stay close to home do not need mercy, but the city where I live has thousands of children in need of kindness. "Go." Most of the children at our church have their physical needs met, but there are thousands in our county who are hungry and in need of clothing. "Go." My boys and their friends have been well provided for, but not all children are so fortunate. "Go." Mercy calls for action, moving, finding, seeking out, looking for. There are children all along the road of life. Some are like the dirty beggar boy outside St. Isaac's. Some are the kids of that woman in Nashville who had no furniture. The good Samaritans find them.

Go and do likewise.

Exercises

Hear A Child

1. Share an example of a time you were extended mercy. What was your reaction?

2. Tell about a time you did not show mercy to a child.

Hear God's Heart

3. Discuss how mercy is the common element in both the story of the prodigal son and the good Samaritan.

4. In Luke 6:36 Jesus says, "Be merciful as your father is merciful." Look through the rest of Luke and write down every situation in which you find Jesus showing mercy. Did Jesus give or deny people dignity?

Hear the Call

5. Why do some people show mercy so easily and others find it so difficult?

6. Talk about a time when you have seen mercy have the following results:
   - Unite people
   - Be aggressive
   - Save lives

7. In Luke 10 the lawyer asks, "Who is my neighbor?" Make your own list of "neighbors" to whom you can show mercy.

8. Discuss ways in which your church or Bible class can be more aggressive in showing mercy.

Chapter Thirteen
Close To Your Heart

Hear the Call

Of the thirteen sad and troubling stories told in the boxes scattered throughout this book and the five discussed in the introduction, ten of them already have a happier ending. April's mother, Sharon, went to prison when April was one year old, but through the grace of God, she found Christ and now the two of them are sitting in our assembly every Sunday. In an unjust and merciless world, she's found fairness and love.

The two teenagers who felt so ostracized when they quit the exclusive club are the girls who worked with me door-knocking in the inner city. I notice that whenever a new teen comes to our church, these two girls provide a warm welcome. They insist that nobody be left out. The 21-year-old former convict is Jeremy, one of the strongest adult workers in our youth ministry. He has blessed our family by his friendship with our younger son.

⊗ ⊘

These Children Mean the World to God

A deacon and I despaired at how we would help a mother tell her eight-year-old Emily and ten-year-old Seth that their dad was into internet pornography and adult clubs and would not be coming home anymore. It was the third such case in less than a month. I felt stretched as far as I could go.

The Ukrainian baby in the Kiev Children's Hospital is alive and well. Antibiotics from Memphis saved the infant's life. Two Christian teens reached out to Marty who came back to Christ. He and I recently presented the Sunday morning lesson together. That's just five of the ten, but their stories make the same point: In helping children, we change the world around us.

But what about the eight sad stories without a happy ending? What about all the children we do not help? What about the children who are shot today? What about the teenager in the suburbs who is at this moment writing a note to her single mother to say that she is running away? How do we help others hear God's heartbeat for children?

The response we often make is to count our blessings and ignore the pain of others. Having gone through difficult times, we move on, rather than showing the way to those who follow. The noise of our own rejoicing often drowns out the cries of children around us. Having brought our own children to safety, we conclude our work is done and never listen for the children that continue to cry. But every blessing carries with it an obligation to be like God.

Another response is to work harder. We put in more hours and make more calls and try to rescue more children. We wear ourselves out. But we can only do so much. Like paint, if we are spread too thinly, we don't cover anything very well. Working harder conveniently narrows the field to the children who fall under our shadow. By focusing on the children served in our ministry, we inadvertently ignore others. Even for people who deeply care for children, "out of sight, out of mind" is an ugly but sadly appropriate proverb.

Sometimes we respond with rigidity. Elders issue dictates to Sunday school teachers to indoctrinate the young people. We think that what worked with one child will be effective with every child or that what pushed one child off the edge will destroy the life of every child. In our attempt to be comprehensive, we overlook the individual cries of each child. We try to make every child fit a mold and in the process create a form that suits few children.

Jesus faced the same situation. There were more blind people than he had sight to give, more hungry folks that he had bread, more lame legs than he had replacement ligaments. Clearly, Jesus didn't lack the power or the resources, but more than once he left hurting people in the crowd because he knew that thin paint wouldn't cover the task before him. What he did do was to inspire those around him to take up the same vision. Through those he enlisted to his cause he accomplished more than he could have humanly done alone.

Hear God's Heart

Our task is not only to hear the cries of the children around us, but to keep God's vision for children alive. Children mean the world to him. When we imitate God, we reach out to children. By changing a child we do a small part in transforming our community. By keeping the vision of hearing the cries of children alive in the spiritual community, we change the world.

How do we keep the dream alive? Can one person make a difference? A series of events in the Old Testament shows us what can happen when just one person helps a child. It is the story of a young man named Hezekiah.

According to 2 Kings 18:1-2 Hezekiah became king in Jerusalem when he was 25 and ruled for the next twenty-nine years. The rest of the chapter tells us about what he did as king, but before we can understand the last twenty-nine years, we need to think about the first twenty-five.

Hezekiah was raised in the royal house by his parents, Ahaz and Abijah. The environment was filled with selfishness, paganism, and oppression. When Hezekiah was nine, his father Ahaz became king. Ahaz was not a man of God. His motto in life seemed to be "Do what's best for Ahaz." He is the only king in Jerusalem who ever closed down the temple and stopped the worship of God. He served whichever pagan god promised the most help (2 Chronicles 28:23). God was so unhappy with Ahaz that he sent the prophet Isaiah to meet with the king in the lower part of the city. Few people in history have had a message delivered directly from God as Ahaz did. Ahaz refused to obey. Apparently, he was doing what was best for Ahaz.

Hezekiah's mother was Abijah, sometimes called Abi. One day Ahaz and Abi came to where their children were playing and took two of Hezekiah's siblings to the valley near Jerusalem and burned them alive. We shudder at the thought, but the king was again doing what was best for Ahaz.

Hezekiah was raised in a pagan home, by a selfish, egotistical father, living in fear that he might be the next child sacrificed in the valley. He grew up in an oppressive, violent, greedy society that routinely ignored the will of God. But when Hezekiah became king, listen to what he did:

> He did what was right in the eyes of the LORD, just as his father David had done. He removed the high places, smashed the sacred stones and cut down the Asherah poles. He broke into pieces the bronze snake Moses had made, for up to that time the Israelites had been burning incense to it. . . . Hezekiah trusted in the LORD, the God of Israel. There was no one like him among all the kings of Judah, either before him or after him. He held fast to the LORD and did not cease to follow him; he kept the commands the LORD had given Moses. And the LORD was with him; he was successful in whatever he undertook. He rebelled against the king of Assyria and did not serve him (2 Kings 18:3-7).

The new king, just twenty-five years old, made radical changes in society, restored temple worship, and led the nation back to

God. A boy raised in a pagan environment changed the face of Jerusalem. The young king did the exact opposite of his father.

Why?

What brought about such a change? Where did Hezekiah learn the ways of God? How could a boy raised in paganism and fear be so bold and godly at the age of twenty-five? Why did a boy reared by parents with selfish values turn out to be a man of godly goals?

The text in 2 Kings does not answer that question, but those who study all the events taking place at this time do have a suggestion. It was because of Micah, a prophet from the countryside who moved to Hezekiah's hometown, who preached barefoot and naked (Micah 1:8), calling for an end to oppression and a return to God. Micah, now known as one of the Minor Prophets, appeared on the scene for just a moment. Many of us don't know much about him, but apparently one young man, a teenager at the time, heard what Micah said. According to Micah 7:1-7, the prophet believed that his mission had failed. It may have been a decade later that the thoughts he planted in Hezekiah's young mind became the restoration experienced under the leadership of one of Judah's greatest kings. One man changed a child. Once Hezekiah was changed, the whole nation changed.

That's the way it is with us. Sometimes we think things can't get any worse. We despair at the school shootings, divorces, alcoholism, runaways, poverty, and racism all around us. The stories in the boxes leave us frustrated and depressed. Then God sends a Micah to stand in the gap. He changes the course of a child's life, and that child goes on to change the whole community.

Hear the Call

God can use each of us just as he used Micah. In our own way, we carry the vision God has for children. In influencing one child, we are part of God changing the whole world. I believe there are people all around us that God is using just like Micah to change the lives of children. Let me tell you about three people who have been Micahs in our community.

Michelle Betts leads our children's ministry. Keeping classes and activities going on Sunday morning and night and again on Wednesday evening involves a great deal of wear and tear. Not long ago the constant effort wore through and the pressure started tearing at her soul. After prayer and seeking the counsel of others, she called a meeting of all the parents of young children in the congregation. The program began with a video one father had taken of children in classes and other activities. Then each parent was asked to write down a Scripture that best expressed the hopes they had for their own children and the other youngsters in our congregation. On another card, they wrote out a prayer for our children's ministry. Michelle then brought out a funnel.

She held it upside down and said, "This is how the children's ministry looks right now: narrow at the top with so much to do at the bottom. How much can go into the funnel this way? Not much!" Then she turned the funnel over. "Our funnel should be like this with the wide part at the top. All of us can work to help our children."

The response to that day has been remarkable. One family told Michelle that they would completely handle arrangements for a major children's program. Five mothers came up and said, "I want to teach." Vacancies that had existed in the Children's Sunday School for months were filled in one day.

What was Michelle doing? She was creating a vision for what God could do through us for children in our city.

Buster Clemens and Donnie Stover lead our youth ministry. In so many places teenagers are viewed as a problem, and the teenage years are seen as a series of rapids to be navigated, a time when you hope you can hold your breath long enough to come safely out on the other side. These two men were not satisfied with that perspective on teens. They view the teen years as a time of opportunity. They have directed us in helping teenagers to be servants, instructing them in showing mercy, and teaching them how to lead their peers to Christ. Donnie and Buster have a vision for teenagers. I have watched them work for over a decade. Their vision for teens is contagious. More than sixty-five adults work with teenagers every week in our congregation. Some parents pick teenagers up from school on Wednesday, feed them supper, and bring them to Wednesday night church! One man met some unchurched teenagers at our school store and now drives fifty miles every Wednesday night to bring those boys to church.

What have Donnie and Buster done? They have created a vision. They have told a story of what God wants Memphis teenagers to be, and it has been contagious. Their passion and goals are now shared by dozens of others so that more teenagers are being influenced for good than any of us could do individually.

I know that Michelle, Buster, and Donnie don't feel like they lead the perfect ministries, but they have learned the lesson of what Micah did for Hezekiah. By changing children, we change the world. By hearing the cries of children and responding as God would, we transform the future through the power of God. Let me tell you why their ministry has a special place in my heart.

Hear a Child

It was Sunday after church in July 1994. I was reading the Sunday paper after having preached that morning. Sally was finishing up the dishes from lunch. Our two sons were playing, or so I thought. My oldest son, Daniel, came into the family room so quietly that his presence momentarily shocked me when I looked up from the paper to find him there.

"Can we talk, Dad?"

"Sure."

"I want to be baptized."

It was a moment that I had waited for ever since we thought about having children, yet when it came I found myself more unprepared than I expected. I imagined that the day my son came to Christ would be an exciting event with family and friends gathered round in great celebration. I had images of people breaking out in song and everyone gathering to celebrate. Instead it came as I was reading the comics.

I'd often worried that my son would not come to Christ, that since he was the preacher's son the pressure might be too much for him, or that for some other reason he would not come to faith. As all worriers do, I dwelt on an unhappy ending to the story so much that the happy ending caught me by surprise. As Daniel stood there I also felt a tinge of guilt that I was one of the fortunate fathers whose child would take up the faith. All these thoughts rushed through my mind as we embraced. I awkwardly tried to express the joy and peace that I felt in my heart, letting him know how happy I was without making it my moment rather than his, without taking over the conversation that he had so bravely begun. After talking about when he would be baptized, I asked him a question.

"Why have you made this decision?"

He said that four things prompted him. First, he and his mother had recently completed a Bible study together. Sally led him through a number of scriptures about salvation and they discussed the numerous conversion stories in the Bible. She had raised issues. He had asked questions. Every Tuesday night for a month they met at the kitchen table while our younger son, Nathan, and I raced toy cars or played repeated games of "Sorry."© Daniel reported that the study had clarified issues about baptism for him and helped him make his decision.

Second, he talked about Christian Camp. Lige, Susan, Buster, and Michelle yearly lead our children in a week of camp. Older kids adopt younger ones. Camp is a "we-must-not-miss-it" event at our house. That year Daniel felt loved and accepted at camp. His cabin counselor, Tommy, had created a warm environment.

Donnie and Jerry mentored him. The boys experienced an uncommon camaraderie, and the whole camp was a grand achievement of Christian fellowship. Daniel loved it and whatever would keep him locked into that kind of ongoing life experience was what he wanted.

Daniel said the third factor was Power Hour. Our teenagers went as a group every week into our inner city. Accompanied by adults they would gather up children in one of the public housing projects in order to teach them about God. Daniel hardly missed a Power Hour. Sometimes he would be an actor in a skit. Other times he led crafts. More recently he had joined with a couple of other teens in leading singing. He said that being with poor children had taught him about life. He saw how fortunate he was to have a stable family and a supportive church. The diversity of life fascinated and informed him. No doubt he could not articulate it at the time, but he was developing a sense of fairness, learning to show mercy, removing prejudicial attitudes, and understanding how to forgive. Such lessons prompted him to think about his own need for God's mercy, his own quest for forgiveness. In doing for the unfortunate of our city, God had taught him about life.

So far I was impressed. I couldn't imagine what more could have prompted him to embrace God. So I waited. What was number four?

He concluded by saying the last thing that led him to baptism was his dad's preaching. Certain muscles in my throat contracted to the point that I could not venture a follow-up question. It occurred to me that he was just saying that to please me, but the look on his face said otherwise. It was a moment of candor between father and son. He had learned to be a son from me as a father, but he had learned the broad principles of the Christian faith from me as a preacher. Preaching makes a difference. God's son was a preacher. It is a noble occupation. I never felt more noble than that July day.

Hear the Call

One concrete result of the work of Michelle, Buster, and Donnie is my own son's conversion to Christ. But there is more. He now has a vision for his own life. In the wonderful environment of the Highland church, my own son has made the same journey that I made. I was born in 1950 and came to Christ in 1964. My own son was born in 1980 and came to Christ in 1994. Daniel's decision was a concrete expression in my life of what this book is about in the life of the church. When my own son came to Christ, it was not only God hearing the cry of another child, but it was also a passing on of the vision. My own son's spiritual life has been touched by the cry of hurting children. Raised in a church that puts special focus on helping children, the mission has touched his heart. Now as a college student, he has composed this song:

Close to Your Heart
And the children play and the children laugh
And the streets are filled with the joy of their love.
And the fathers and mothers look down on their children
And lovingly hold them close to their hearts.

A boy named Jason has no one to raise him:
He never laughs and he's never loved.
His parents died when he was a toddler
And his only parent is a government home.

Sergei and Tonya were whipped by their father;
Their mother would love them when she wasn't drunk.
Their teacher was racist and said they were worthless,
So they hold to each other in fear for their lives.

Nana is five and raised by her sisters.
When they're doing well, she gets one meal a day.
And this third-world country can't even clothe her
But listen to her and this child will say . . .

That the children play and the children laugh
And the streets are filled with the joy of their love.
'Cause the Father above looks down on his children
and lovingly holds them close to his heart.

Sergei and Tonya, Nana and Jason
Have a Father who'll love them forever.
Because he loves them he asks you, his children,
To lovingly hold them close to your hearts.

What my son sings is what I have tried to write. I was a lonely child who struggled to find someone to listen. Then I developed a deafness to the cries of children when I became an adult. One of the major turns in my adult life was when I turned back to hear the cries of children. Now my own son hears those same cries and sings what I preach.

The vision is not his or mine. It doesn't belong to Michelle, Donnie, or Buster. It belongs to our Lord. Children mean the world to God. It is the vision of a God who heard the cry of Ishmael. It's the compassion of the father who listened to the boy who left, and the one who stayed. It's the heartbeat of the one who sent Micah to transform the life of a young monarch-to-be named Hezekiah.

Children are crying. God hears and because we know he hears, it moves us to listen. When we listen, God moves us to respond. Through our actions, God transforms the life of a child. As the church hears and responds to the cries of children, an amazing thing happens. Through a ministry to children, we begin to change the whole world.

Exercises

Hear A Child

1. Which of the stories in the margins of this book touched you?

2. Tell of a child you know who has God's heart for other children.

Hear God's Heart

3. How did you feel when you heard about the nature of Hezekiah's childhood? What do you think prepared him to be a good king?

4. Read Micah 7:1-7. Do you think Micah was discouraged?

Hear the Call

5. How does your church advocate God's vision for children in your community?

6. How does your church minister to children? Besides ministries in the church, give specific examples.

Appendix
Selected Child Care Organizations Listed by State

Alabama

Agape of Central Alabama
Montgomery, AL   (334) 272-9466
Agape of North Alabama, Inc.
Huntsville, AL   (256) 859-4481
Florence, AL   (256) 767-1084
Childhaven, Inc.
Cullman, AL   (256) 734-6720
Christian Children's Home
Florence, AL   (256) 757-4212
Community Thrift Store
Gadsden, AL   (256) 543-1888

Arkansas

Agape Child And Family Services, Inc.
Memphis, TN   (901) 323-3600
Children's Home, Inc.
Paragould, AR   (870) 239-4031
Searcy Children's Home, Inc.
Searcy, AR   (501) 268-3243
Southern Christian Home
Morrilton, AR   (501) 354-2428

California
Agape Villages, Inc.,
Sierra Children's Home
Dublin, CA   (925) 829-7211
City of Children
Norco, CA   (909) 734-1086
Mexico Office   01152-617-46048
Hillview Acres Children's Home
Chino, CA   (909) 628-1272

Colorado
Colorado Christian Services
Englewood, CO   (303) 761-7236
Mountain States Children's Home
Longmont, CO   (303) 776-6841

Delaware
Aletheia Child Care
Newark, DE   (302) 737-3781

Florida
Christian Family Services, Inc.
Gainesville, FL   (352) 378-6202
Christian Home and Bible School
Mt. Dora, FL   (352) 383-2155
Christian Homes for Children, Inc.
Hialeah, FL   (305) 825-0517

Georgia
Christian Family Services
Ringold, GA   (706) 935-9961
Georgia Agape, Inc.
Atlanta, GA   (770) 452-9995
North Georgia Christian Family Services, Inc.
Athens, GA   (706) 769-0601
Raintree Village, Inc., The Children's Home
Valdosta, GA   (912) 559-5944

Illinois
Christian Family Services, Inc.
Fairview Heights, IL   (618) 397-7678

Indiana
Childplace
Jeffersonville, IN   (812) 282-8248
Shults-Lewis Child & Family Services, Inc.
Valparaiso, IN   (219) 462-0513
Southeastern Children's Home
Indianapolis, IN   (317) 352-9296

Kansas
Christian Family Services of the Midwest, Inc.
Overland Park, KS   (913) 383-3337
Maude Carpenter Children's Center
Wichita, KS   (316) 942-3221

Kentucky
  Childplace
  Louisville, KY   (502) 363-1633
  Lexington, KY   (606) 255-2520
  New Pathways For Children, Inc.
  Melber, KY   (502) 443-9754
  Potter Children's Home, Inc.
  Bowling Green, KY   (502) 843-3038
Mississippi
  Agape Child And Family Services, Inc.
  Memphis, TN   (901) 323-3600
  Christians in Action, Inc.
  Jackson, MS   (601) 353-1942
  Pinevale Children's Home
  Corinth, MS   (662) 286-6555
  Sunnybrook Children's Home
  Jackson, MS   (601) 856-6555
Missouri
  Children's Homes
  Kennett, MO   (573) 888-3627
  Christian Family Services, Inc.
  St. Louis, MO   (314) 968-2216
  Christian Family Services of The Midwest, Inc.
  Kansas City, MO   (816) 763-4230
  Fairhaven Children's Home
  Strafford, MO   (417) 862-6675
Nebraska
  Nebraska Christian Services, Inc,
  Omaha, NE   (402) 334-3278
New Hampshire
  Country Acres of New England
  Gilsum, NH   (603) 352-5506
New Mexico
  Albuquerque Christian Children's Home
  Albuquerque, NM   (505) 898-5520
  Manuelito Navajo Children's Home, Inc.
  Gallup, NM   (505) 863-5530
  New Mexico Christian Children's Home
  Portales, NM   (505) 356-5372
New York
  Timothy Hill Children's Ranch, Inc.
  Riverhead, NY   (631) 369-1234
North Carolina
  Agape of North Carolina, Inc.
  Greensboro, NC   (910) 855-7107

Ohio
   Mid-Western Children's Home
   Pleasant Plain, OH   (513) 877-2141
Oklahoma
   Colorado Christian Services of Oklahoma
   Oklahoma City, OK   (405) 478-3362
   Hope Harbor
   Claremore, OK   (918) 343-0003
   The Tipton Home
   Tipton, OK   (580) 667-5221
South Carolina
   Southeastern Children's Home, Inc.
   Duncan, SC   (864) 439-0259
Tennessee
   Agape, Inc.
   Nashville, TN   (615) 781-3000
   Agape Child And Family Services, Inc.
   Memphis, TN   (901) 323-3600
   Agape Child And Family Services, Inc.
   Jackson, TN   (901) 668-9698
   East Tennessee Christian Services, Inc.
   Knoxville, TN   (865) 584-0841
   Greater Chattanooga Christian Services, Inc.
   Chattanooga, TN   (423) 756-0281
   Happy Haven Homes, Inc.
   Cookeville, TN   (931) 526-2052
   Madison Children's Home And Domestic Violence Program
   Madison, TN   (615) 860-4461
   Tennessee Children's Home
   Spring Hill, TN   (931) 486-2274
   North Central Tennessee
   (Formerly Happy Hills Youth Ranch)
   Ashland City, TN   (615) 307-3205
   West Tennessee (Formerly West Tennessee Children's Home)
   Pinson, TN   (901) 989-7335
Texas
   Boles Children's Home
   Quinlan, TX   (903) 883-2204
   Central Texas Children's Home
   Austin, TX   (512) 918-2824
   Cherokee Home For Children
   Cherokee, TX   (915) 622-4201
   Children's Home of Lubbock And Family Services Agency,
   Inc.
   Lubbock, TX   (806) 762-0481
   Texas Boys' Ranch (Sub-site of Children's Home of Lubbock)
   Lubbock, TX   (806) 747-3187

Christian Child Help Foundation
Houston, TX   (713) 681-6900
Christian Homes of Abilene, Inc.
Abilene, TX   (915) 677-2205
Christian Relief Fund
Amarillo, TX   (806) 352-5030
Christian Services of The Southwest
Dallas, TX   (972) 960-9981
Christ's Haven For Children
Keller, TX   (817) 431-1544
High Plains Children's Home & Family Services, Inc.
Amarillo, TX   (806) 622-2272
Medina Children's Home
Medina, TX   (830) 589-2871
Sherwood And Myrtie Foster's Home For Children
Stephenville, TX   (254) 968-2143
Smithlawn Maternity Home And Adoption Agency
Lubbock, TX   (806) 745-2574
Sunny Glen Children's Home
San Benito, TX   (956) 399-5356
Virginia
Rainbow Christian Services
Gainesville, VA   (703) 754-8516
Washington
Church of Christ Homes For Children
Federal Way, WA   (253) 839-2758
West Virginia
Childplace
Charleston, WV   (304) 757-0763

Selected Organizations Ministering to Children and Families

Aim for Success   www.aimforsuccess.org
Christian Child and Family Services   www.ccfsa.org
Christian Relief Fund   www.christianrelieffund.org
Compassion International   www.compassion.com
Doug Fields   www.youthministryonline.com
Feed the Children   www.feedthechildren.org
Focus on the Family   (800) AFAMILY or www.family.org
Group Publishing   www.grouppublishing.com
Manna International   (800) 253-2420
National Conference on Youth Ministries   ww.ncym.org
Workcamp for Teenagers   bclemens@highlandcc.org
Youth Specialties   www.youthspecialties.com

Selected Resources on Ministering to Children and Families

Choun, Robert J. and Michael S. Lawson. *The Christian Educator's Handbook on Children's Ministry.* Grand Rapids: Baker Books, 1998.

Johnson, Susanne. *Christian Spiritual Formation in the Church and Classroom.* Nashville: Abingdon, 1989.

LeBar, Lois E. *Children in the Bible School.* Westwood: Fleming H. Revell, 1962.

Richards, Larry. *A Theology of Children's Ministry.* Grand Rapids: Zondervan, 1983.

Children's Ministry Magazine	(970) 669-3836
Church and Family Magazine	ICF@Harding.edu
21st Century Christian Magazine	(800) 331-5991
Our Families Magazine	www.faulkner.edu

Selected Sources on the Theology of Children

Beasley-Murray, George R. "The Theology of the Child," *American Baptist Quarterly* 2 (December 1982) 197-202.

Bunge, Marcia J., ed. *The Child in Christian Thought.* Grand Rapids: Eerdmans, 2001.

Dawn, Marva J. *Is It A Lost Cause? Having the Heart of God for the Church's Children.* Grand Rapids: Eerdmans, 1997.

Hendricks, William L. *A Theology for Children.* Nashville: Broadman Press, 1980.

Morgenthaler, Sally, ed.. *Exploring Children's Spiritual Formation: Foundational Issues.* River Forest, IL: Pillars Press, 1999.

Scalise, Pamela. "'I Have Produced a Man with the Lord': God as Provider of Offspring in Old Testament Theology," *Review & Expositor* 91 (1994) 577-589.

Schultze, Quentin J. *Winning Your Kids Back From the Media.* Downers Grove: InterVarsity Press, 1994.

Stewart, Sonja M., and Jerome W. Berryman. *Young Children and Worship.* Louisville: Westminster/John Knox Press, 1989.

Stonehouse, Catherine. *Joining Children on the Spiritual Journey.* Grand Rapids: Baker Books, 1998.

Thorburn, Marjorie. *The Spirit of The Child.* London: George Allen and Unwin Ltd, 1946.

Weber, Hans-Ruedi. "Jesus and the Children," *Biblical Resources for Study and Preaching.* Atlanta: John Knox Press, 1979.

Wright-Edelman, Marian. "A Call for Compassion and Justice: Rescuing Our Nation's Children and Their Families," *Review and Expositor* 91 (1994) 309-324.

Yoder, Marvin K. *What We Believe About Children.* Scottdale, PA: Herald Press, 1984.

Zuck, Roy B. *Precious in His Sight: Childhood and Children in the Bible.* Grand Rapids, MI: Baker, 1996.